D1241102

THE SUMERIAN PROBLEM

MAJOR ISSUES IN HISTORY

Editor
C. WARREN HOLLISTER,
University of California, Santa Barbara

C. Warren Hollister: *The Twelfth-Century Renaissance*
William F. Church: *The Impact of Absolutism in France: National Experience under Richelieu, Mazarin, and Louis XIV*
C. Warren Hollister: *The Impact of the Norman Conquest*
Roger L. Williams: *The Commune of Paris, 1871*
L. Pearce Williams: *Relativity Theory: Its Origins and Impact on Modern Thought*
Loy Bilderback: *Conciliarism*
Robert O. Collins: *The Partition of Africa: Illusion or Necessity*
J. B. Conacher: *The Emergence of Parliamentary Democracy in Britain in the 19th Century*
Frank J. Frost: *Democracy and the Athenians*
Paul Hauben: *The Spanish Inquisition*
Bennett D. Hill: *Church and State in the Middle Ages*
Boyd H. Hill: *The Rise of the First Reich: Germany in the Tenth Century*
Thomas M. Jones: *The Becket Controversy*
Tom B. Jones: *The Sumerian Question*
Anthony Molho: *Social and Economic Foundations of the Italian Renaissance*
E. W. Monter: *European Witchcraft*
Donald Queller: *The Latin Conquest of Constantinople*
Jeffrey Russell: *Medieval Religions Dissent*
Arthur J. Slavin: *Humanism, Reform, and Reformation*
W. Warren Wagar: *The Idea of Progress Since the Renaissance*

THE SUMERIAN PROBLEM

EDITED BY

Tom Jones

Professor of History
University of Minnesota
Minneapolis, Minnesota

John Wiley & Sons, Inc.

New York   London   Sydney   Toronto

SERIES PREFACE

Traditionally, the reading program in a history survey course has usually consisted of a large two-volume textbook and, perhaps, a book of readings. This simple reading program requires few decisions and little imagination on the instructor's part, and tends to encourage in the student the virtue of careful memorization. Such programs are by no means things of the past, but they certainly do not represent the wave of the future.

The reading program in survey courses at many colleges and universities today is far more complex. At the risk of over simplification, and allowing for many exceptions and overlaps, it can be divided into four categories: (1) textbook, (2) original source readings, (3) specialized historical essays and interpretive studies, and (4) historical problems.

Having obtained an overview of the course subject matter (textbook), having sampled the original sources, and having been exposed to selective examples of excellent modern historical writing (historical essays), the student can turn to the crucial task of weighing various possible interpretations of major historical issues. It is at this point that memory gives way to creative critical thought. The "problems approach," in other words, is the intellectual climax to a thoughtfully conceived reading program and is, indeed, the most characteristic of all approaches to historical pedagogy among the newer generation of college and university teachers.

The historical problems books currently available are many and varied. Why add to this information explosion? Because the Wiley "Major Issues" series constitutes an endeavor to produce something new that will respond to pedagogical needs thus far unmet. To begin with, it is a series of individual volumes—one per problem. Many good teachers would much prefer to select their own historical issues rather than be tied to an inflexible sequence of issues imposed by a publisher and bound together between two covers. Second, the Wiley "Major Issues" series is based on the idea of approaching the significant problems of history through a deft interweaving of primary sources and secondary analysis, fused together by the skill of a scholar-editor. It is felt that the essence of an historical issue cannot be satisfactorily probed either by placing a body of undigested source materials into the hands of inexperienced students or by limiting these students to the controversial literature of modern scholars who debate the meaning of sources that the student never sees. The "Major Issues" series approaches historical problems by exposing students to both the finest historical thinking on the issue and some of the evidence on which this thinking is based. This synthetic approach should prove far more fruitful than either the raw-source approach or the exclusively second-hand approach, for it combines the advantages —and avoids the serious disadvantages—of both.

Finally, the editors of the individual volumes in the "Major Issues" series have been chosen from among the ablest scholars in their fields. Rather than faceless referees, they are historians who know their issues from the inside and, in most instances, have themselves contributed significantly to the relevant scholarly literature. It has been the editorial policy of this series to permit the editor-scholars of the individual volumes the widest possible latitude both in formulating their topics and in organizing their materials. Their scholarly competence has been unquestioningly respected; they have been encouraged to approach the problems as they see fit. The titles and themes of the series volumes have been suggested in nearly every case by the scholar-editors themselves. The criteria have been (1) that the issue be of relevance to undergraduate lecture courses in history, and (2) that it be an issue that the scholar-editor knows thoroughly and in which he has done creative work. And, in general, the second criterion has been given precedence over the first. In short, the question, "What are the significant historical issues today?" has been answered not by general editors or sales departments but by the scholar-teachers who are responsible for these volumes.

C. Warren Hollister

University of California
Santa Barbara

PREFACE

To study the Sumerian Problem is to survey more than a century of scholarship. It discloses the progression from the talented amateur of the nineteenth century to the fearsome specialist of the middle twentieth; for those who will learn, it has much to teach about logic; and it reveals to the outsider something of the closed society of the Assyriologists.

Those familiar with this series will find that this book does not conform in every detail to the usual format. The reason for this is that the scholars who wrote about the Sumerian Problem seldom had the general reader in mind but, instead, sought to communicate with each other. It was, therefore, necessary to substitute an extended commentary for some highly technical material.

Even reduced to its simplest terms, as in this text, the Sumerian Problem is hard sledding, but as an eye-opener for the layman with intellectual curiosity the experience may be worth it. *Caveat lector!*

I wish to express my gratitude to Professors John Brinkman and Erle Leichty, who read my manuscript and made several helpful suggestions.

Tom B. Jones

CONTENTS

Contents

THE SUMERIAN PROBLEM

Introduction: The Sumerian Problem

During the third millennium (3000–2000) B.C. many of the basic elements destined to be characteristic of the civilization of Mesopotamia for centuries to come were created and elaborated by a people called the Sumerians. In religion, literature, art, architecture, mathematics, astronomy, political theory, law, and economic organization, their contributions were fundamental for subsequent developments. Not only did the Sumerians give form to civilization in their own territory in the lower Tigris-Euphrates valley, but also numerous culture traits of Sumerian origin were borrowed and adapted by their contemporaries and by later peoples in both neighboring and remote regions. Iraq Iran, Anatolia, Syria, and Palestine were affected; Sumerian culture reached and influenced even Egypt and the Aegean lands; and forty centuries and thousands of miles removed from the Sumerians and their homeland, our own civilization still retains cultural items of ultimate Sumerian origin.

Because all of the archaeological materials as well as thousands of Sumerian inscriptions and texts of various kinds have not been fully studied and their evidence synthesized, and because we know that future excavations will disclose more evidence, the full contribution of the Sumerians to civilization cannot yet be measured. Moreover, there are even more elementary things about the Sumerians that are still unknown. For over a century scholars have tried to find answers for several questions:

Who were the Sumerians? Where did they come from? When did they arrive in Mesopotamia? Did they initiate the development of culture there, or did they build upon foundations provided by earlier inhabitants?

All these questions are comprehended in what is called "The Sumerian Problem." Naturally a matter of concern to students of ancient history, the Sumerian Problem in all of its ramifications has an even wider value and interest because it is representative of a familiar type of historical question. Its story includes most of the classic elements: recognition of the existence of a problem, early attempts at solution by proceeding from the assumed known to the admitted unknown, the application of various problem-solving techniques and methods derived from a variety of disciplines, and the chameleon-like changes in the aspects of the question brought about by new discoveries and increased awareness of the complexities of the problem. Replete with magnificent examples of human ingenuity and marred by the usual instances of academic rivalry and competition, the history of the Sumerian Problem is long and varied. Still unsolved, it may be incapable of solution.

The famous Homeric Question and our Sumerian Problem have more than a little in common. In both cases, the initial study was made by philologists; then the archaeologists arrived on the scene to clarify some points and confuse others. In both cases, the aid of comparative literature was enlisted; and in both, although at different stages, the decipherment of unknown scripts played a major role. Concepts of the nature and extent of the two problems changed with the passing years, and scholars of various nationalities joined the fray on shifting battlefields. Like the Sumerian Problem, the Homeric Question has not been laid to rest.

PART ONE
The First Phase: Philology

Civilizations rise and fall; sometimes they vanish. In the last one hundred years a few lost civilizations have been found: prime examples are those of the Minoans, the Indus Valley people, and the Sumerians. Archaeologists uncovered the Minoan and Indus civilizations, but philologists happened upon the Sumerians—quite by accident.

It all began with the successful decipherment of the cuneiform. This ancient system of writing with its wedge-shaped or "arrow-headed" characters had aroused the curiosity of European travelers in Iran and Iraq as early as the seventeenth century. By 1800, it was generally recognized that inscribed stones found in southwestern Iran (Persia) often bore texts in three different varieties of cuneiform writing. Moreover, the least complex kind of the cuneiform seemed to occur mostly on Persian sites, while the other two appeared to have a wider geographical distribution. It was, therefore, assumed that the first variety had as its underlying language a dialect of Persian, probably that used by the Achaemenid kings of the line of Cyrus the Great and the equally great Darius (*c.* 550–330 B.C.). Proceeding on these assumptions and adding the hypothesis that the nearly two score characters of the Persian cuneiform represented a kind of alphabet, George Grotefend, a German schoolmaster, achieved a partial decipherment of this script at the beginning of the nineteenth century. In less than fifty years, the work begun by Grotefend had been essentially completed by the Englishman, H.C. Rawlinson, who had risked his life to secure copies of the great Bisitun Inscription carved in the three cunei-

3

form scripts high on the side of a mountain northeast of Baghdad.[1]

The value of the Bisitun text was that it was very long. Every character of the Persian script occurred many times—this was not true of the shorter inscriptions found in Persia itself—and thus Rawlinson and others now had ample opportunity to test the assumptions that they made about the phonetic values of the characters and to be sure that these values could be consistently applied. This, of course, is the acid test to which every decipherment must be subjected in order to determine its validity.

The decipherment of the Persian brand of cuneiform was a relatively simple matter for three reasons. First, the system of writing was not complex, and its characters were few in number. Second, since Persian had survived as a modern living language, it was possible to go back from it to the Old Persian and reconstruct the ancient forms. Third, the names of the Achaemenid kings—Cyrus, Cambyses, Darius, Xerxes, Artaxerxes, and the rest which occurred many times in the inscriptions—were already familiar from the classical Greco-Roman accounts. In addition, since Herodotus had provided a version of the events surrounding the accession of Darius the Great, his account was helpful in translating the Bisitun inscription that dealt with the same subject.

Now, the Bisitun inscription had an additional virtue: it was a *trilingual*. That is, its texts told the same story in three different languages; and, of course, each language was written in a different cuneiform script. This meant that once the Persian script and text could be read, work could progress on the decipherment of the other two scripts. The system employed by both the remaining types of cuneiform was obviously very complex, for they used hundreds of characters as opposed to the limited number involved in the Persian variety. It had to be assumed that the two undeciphered scripts resembled the Japanese or the then newly deciphered Egyptian in which there were not only char-

[1] For an account of the decipherment, see S. N. Kramer, *The Sumerians*, Chicago, 1963, pp. 9–19; T. Jones, *Paths to the Ancient Past*, New York, 1967, pp. 46–69.

acters with phonetic values but also many pictographs and ideo-graphs. Nor could one with confidence make any assumptions about the languages underlying these two scripts, although it did appear from the geographical distribution of the inscriptions that one script belonged to the Tigris-Euphrates valley while the other was largely confined to the region of Susa in the moun-tains just north of Basra.

Many people had been at work on the undeciphered scripts in the twenty years before Rawlinson published his final edition of the Bisitun texts, 1846–1851. Among those so engaged were Edward Hincks of Dublin, Jules Oppert of France, and Rawlin-son himself. Several discoveries emerged which we shall presently consider in detail, but it should be said first of all that the language underlying the "Babylonian" script was found to belong to the Semitic family; it proved to be rather close to Hebrew, Arabic, and other languages well known to scholars long before 1850. The other language, variously called "Scythic" or "Susian," is now known as Elamite; it belongs to a quite different and ob-scure language group that even today cannot be read with facility.

Once the Semitic character of the language underlying the "Babylonian" script had been suspected, the study of the script itself progressed swiftly, for a vast amount of material for analysis lay at hand: there were not only the Babylonian version of the Bisitun text and other inscriptions long known from the lower Tigris-Euphrates valley but there were also the thousands of texts on stone and clay that Layard and Botta had unearthed in Assyria.[2]

The "Babylonian" cuneiform and the Elamite, too, were, as had been expected, found to be far more complicated in opera-tion than the Persian. Yet even the Persian was not, after all, an alphabetic script: it proved to be a syllabary that had char-acters for writing sets of consonant-vowel combinations as well as separate signs for the vowels alone. In a system of this kind there are characters for the vowels— a, e, i, etc.—and char-

[2] For Layard and Botta, see Kramer, *op. cit.*, pp. 7–9; Jones, *op. cit.*, pp. 7–25.

acters for consonant-vowel combinations—ba, bi, bo, ka, ki, ko, ku, and so on. The reader may wish to test his comprehension of this by deciphering the inscription given below in which the system of writing is syllabic and the underlying language, English.

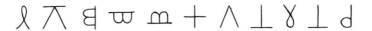

The vowels represented in this text have the values:

> long a (ā, as in bay)
> long e (ē, as in bee)
> long i (ī, as in buy)
> short a (ă, as in bah)
> short i (ĭ, as in bin)

The characters of the syllabary used for the inscription are given in the grid below:

	Ā	Ă	Ē	Ī	Ĭ	TO BE READ
VOWELS ALONE					+	Ĭ
B	ᚳ		ᙢ	ꙗ		BĀ, BĒ, BĪ
K		ㅠ				KĂ
N		Λ				NĂ
P		d				PĂ
R		ℓ	४			RĂ, RĒ
T		⊥				TĂ

The "Babylonian" cuneiform used characters for vowels and syllables, but in addition to consonant-vowel combinations (like the Persian), it used vowel-consonant combinations, too. In this expanded system we could rewrite the inscription given above and introduce new characters.

Thus:

ʅ ⅄ ᗺ ៙ ᒧ ∨ ⊣ ⅄ ⊥ σ

Furthermore, in the Babylonian script there were characters for pictographs and ideographs as well as for the phonetic (syllabic) signs. This was because the cuneiform system of writing was derived from an original that had begun with picture writing (pictographs or iconographic signs); then ideographic signs had been added; and finally the writing had come to the phonetic stage. As in the Egyptian system, however, the earlier pictographs and ideographs had never been discarded but were used along with the phonetic characters. In such a system, one might have a character representing the sea (ocean). This would be a pictograph, but as an ideograph the same character might stand for "to storm," "to drown" or even for "waves" or "salt"—something associated with the sea. Finally, as a phonetic character this identical sign, if the system had originally been devised to write English, would stand for the *sound* see.

Such a system, however, could be adapted for writing more than one language. Using simply pictographs and ideographs, one could write as follows:

And read:

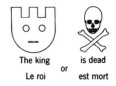

The king   is dead
          or
Le roi   est mort

Adding phonetic characters:

8   *LE*

⊗   *THE*

∀   *Ā (long a)*

Z   *IS*

One might read:

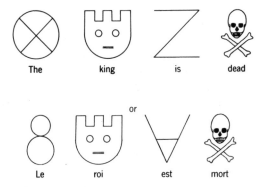

If we continue to imagine that our hypothetical script had been devised for writing English and had then been adapted for writing a different language, we could deduce this fact even if we had not known it at first. The following examples will demonstrate this:

If stands for sea (pictographic)
storm (ideograghic)
sē (phonetic, as in see)

and if stands for eye (pictographic)
to see (ideograghic)
aye (phonetic, as in sigh)

We could write:

I see (ideo) the sea (pict)

or

Je vois   la mer

And we could write:

I (phon) see (ideo) the (phon) sea (pict)

or

I (phon) sē (phon) the (phon) sea (pict)

But we could *not* write "Je vois la mer" *phonetically* with the *same* characters that we used to write "I see the sea." We should have to devise new characters for "je" and "vois" even if

we could create "la" and "mer" from the pictographs

(la) and ⌒ (mare) and use them as phonetic signs. It would thus be apparent from a study of "I see the sea" that the progression from an English original "sea" to phonetic "sē" was possible, while one could not go from a French original "mer" to phonetic "sē." From this and similar examples the English origin of the hypothetical system could thus be discovered.

It was by such a process of reasoning that Edward Hincks in 1850 concluded that the "Babylonian" cuneiform had not been invented by the Semitic-speaking Babylonians and Assyrians. A summary of his remarks to the British Association for the Advancement of Science read as follows:[3]

> Much interesting ethnological information has been already obtained from the Assyrian inscriptions that have been brought to

[3] E. Hincks, "On the Language and Mode of Writing of the Ancient Assyrians," *British Association for the Advancement of Science*, 20 (1850), p. 140.

light; and more may be confidently expected, as these inscriptions shall be discovered. Apart, however, from all such information, the language and the mode of writing of the Assyrians are themselves two important ethnological facts. The language of the Assyrio-Babylonian inscriptions is generally admitted to be of the family called Semitic. It is in many respects strikingly like the Hebrew; but has some peculiarities, which were mentioned, in common with Egyptian, the relationship of which to the Semitic languages has already been recognized. The mode of writing of the Assyrians differed from that of the Hebrew and all other Semitic languages, and agreed with the Egyptian, in that it was partly ideographic. Some words consisted entirely of ideographs; others were written in part phonetically, but had ideographs united with the phonetic part. As to the part of the writing which consisted of phonographs, Dr. Hincks maintained, in opposition to all other writers, that the characters had all definite syllabic values; there being no consonants, and consequently no necessity or liberty of supplying vowels. In proof that the characters had definite syllabic values, he handed about copies of a lithographed plate, in which examples of various forms of words analogous to those existing in Hebrew were collected together. The use of characters representing syllables he considered to be an indication that, though the language of the Assyrians was Semitic, their mode of writing was not so. A second proof of the same position he derived from the absence of distinct syllables to represent combinations of the peculiar Semitic consonants Koph and Ain. From these facts he inferred that the Assyrio-Babylonian mode of writing was adopted from some Indo-European nation, which had probably conquered Assyria; and he thought it likely that this nation had intercourse with the Egyptians, and had, in part at least, derived its mode of writing from that most ancient people.

Hincks was correct in his deduction that the cuneiform was non-Babylonian in origin, but he was mistaken about the Indo-European aspect of the original and also about its indebtedness to the Egyptians. In short, he was trying to relate something unknown to what he and others already knew, or thought they knew. By 1857, when Hincks again addressed himself to the subject, the work of Rawlinson and Oppert had done much to clarify the situation. Their research will be described presently, but we shall content ourselves for the moment with the remark that the language of the inventors of the cuneiform had now been called "Akkadian" by Rawlinson, while much later (1869) Oppert was to give it the correct name of "Sumerian."

Below, in part, is what Hincks said in 1857:[4]

The facts from which the author proposed to reason relate to the language of the Assyrians, the mode of writing of the Assyrians, and the language of the people who invented this mode of writing, or, as they have been called, the Accadians. The Assyrian language is a member of the family which has been generally called Semitic. This term may be retained, as no preferable term presents itself; but is objectionable, as we have no reason to suppose that the divisions of mankind with respect to language and with respect to descent were coincident. All the Semitic languages that were known before the discovery of the Assyrian agree with one another in some important particulars in which they differ from the Assyrian. For example, they have H in the separate pronouns and affixes of the third person, and in the preformative of causative verbs; while the Assyrian has S. They may be classed together as the Syro-Arabian sub-family of the Semitic family of languages; the Assyrio-Babylonian being its other sub-family.

The grand distinctive feature of the Semitic languages is that in them the roots are *consonantal*. Most commonly, they consist of three consonants, or what are considered as such; but in no instance does a *vowel* form part of the root. The vowels are used to determine the grammatical forms, which they sometimes do alone, but oftener with the assistance of consonants, prefixed or suffixed to those of the root or inserted among them. In all other languages, on the contrary, the roots are syllabic; though in many languages the vowels are liable to be changed in certain grammatical forms, and consonants may be inserted within the roots. Besides the

[4] E. Hincks, "On the Relation Between the Newly Discovered Accadian Language and the Indo-European, Semitic, and Egyptian Languages," *British Association for the Advancement of Science*, 27 (1857) pp. 134–138.

ordinary consonants, the semi-vowels W and Y, and certain breath-ings, there are combinations of consonantal sounds, which are treated in Semitic grammar as simple consonants.

Now this distinctive feature of Semitic language, that its roots are consonantal, connects itself naturally with a distinctive feature of Semitic writing. It is consonantal. Its characters represent those consonants, or what were considered as such, which are capable of being elements of roots. It has, properly speaking, no vowels. In Hebrew, as it is now printed, there are points attached to the letters, which indicate the vowels with which these letters are to be sounded; but it is generally admitted that these points were no part of the original text. . . .

All the Semitic languages with which we were acquainted pre-viously to the deciphering of the Assyrio-Babylonian inscriptions were originally written from right to left, and with consonants only; and no languages other than Semitic ones were thus written, except under Semitic influence. It was therefore a natural sup-position that the cuneiform writing of Babylon, where a Semitic language was believed to have been spoken, would be written with characters which represented the Semitic consonants. Two circumstances might have suggested doubts as to this being the case; the writing was directed from left to right, and the characters were far more numerous than in the Semitic alphabet; but not-withstanding these objections, all who undertook the decipher-ment of the inscriptions before 1847, with the single exception of Grotefend, referred the characters to the Semitic alphabet. The explanation which they gave of the large number of characters was that each letter was represented by several equivalent characters; and that some characters represented combinations of letters. . . . Grotefend denied the equivalence of any two characters, and supposed that characters might represent consonants, combina-tions of consonants, vowels or syllables . . . In the latter end of 1847, it occurred to the author of this paper that the characters must represent definite syllables, no character representing a de-tached consonant, and no vowel being left unexpressed. He con-sidered that the Assyrians did not analyze their words beyond syllables; they did not recognize consonants or vowels as constituents of syllables; their characters represented simple syllables or combinations of syllables; not Semitic letters or combinations of them, as the French decipherers and Sir H. Rawlinson supposed, nor European letters and combinations of them, as Grotefend thought. . . .

This, then, being a settled point, it comes to be inquired, how came the Assyrians to write on a totally different system from what all other Semitic people used? The answer to this question given by the author in 1850 was, that the Assyrians learned their system of writing from a non-Semitic people. He then thought that this other people had partially adopted the Egyptian system of writing; but he was now satisfied that they had invented it independently of the Egyptians. What suggested to him that the inventors of cuneatic writing were acquainted with hieroglyphic writing was that the ideographic characters were mixed with phonetic ones in both the systems. This alone, however, would not prove that this was the case; for ideographic characters are mixed with phonetic ones in almost all systems. The Arabic and Roman numerals, the signs for degrees, minutes and seconds, and for the different denominations of money and the like, are ideographic. These have not been borrowed from either the Assyrian or the Egyptian system; why then should it be thought that one of these was borrowed from the other? Unless the ideographs were introduced among the phonographs in a strikingly similar manner in the two systems, it would by no means follow that one system was taken from the other. The author, however, denied that they were introduced in a similar manner. The Egyptians sometimes wrote the name of an object phonetically, and added the figure or symbol of the object; but the Assyrians never did so. They wrote down the word or they wrote down the sign; but they never wrote down both, one after the other. At other times, the Egyptians wrote the name of an object phonetically, and wrote after it the ideograph, not of the object, but of the species of genus to which it belonged. The Assyrians did something like this, but not this. They prefixed the ideographic sign of the species to the name of the individual, or that of the genus to the name of the species. They prefixed what the Egyptians postfixed. Surely, if they had learned the use of determinative signs from the Egyptians, they would have used them as the Egyptians did. Again, compound ideographs are used in Egyptian writing; but though there appear to be instances of the use of them in Assyrian writing, these are capable of a different explanation, which is probably the true one. We have a combination of two characters, which signifies "a son;" the characters signifying severally "child" and "male." Sir Henry Rawlinson has, however, suggested that these characters, which have the phonetic values *tur* and *us*, represent words of the Accadian language to which the cuneatic writing was first applied. These Accadian words, when alone, are interchanged with the equivalent Assyrian words . . . the compound Accadian word *Tur-us*, "male child," is written when the equivalent Assyrian word *pal* should be read . . . a great deal of the supposed ideographic writing of the Assyrians is thus, in fact, a writing down of Accadian words, when the equivalent Assyrian words are to be read; a mode of proceeding which was certainly not learned from the Egyptians, who practiced nothing at all like it. Strange as this mode of proceeding must appear, and as it certainly is, it has some resemblance to what occurs in English. Abbreviations are frequently used, which represent Latin words, and which are nevertheless read by English words. Thus "£, represents "*librae*," but is read "pounds;" "e.g." represents "*exempli gratia*," but is read "for example." It thus appears that so far as respects their use of ideographs, there is very little resemblance between the Assyrian and Egyptian systems of writing; certainly not enough to require us to attribute to them a common origin. Let us now look to the form and values of the characters. In both systems we have representations of "the mouth" and of "water;" but they are as unlike as it would be possible to make them. The Egyptians represented the mouth as seen in front, the Assyrians as seen from the side. . . . The Assyrians represented water by drops of rain; the Egyptians by the waved surface of standing water. Surely there would have not been such differences if one system had been taken from the other. Again, the Egyptian characters for the most part represented incomplete syllables, requiring vowels to be supplied which were not expressed; whereas the

Assyrian characters all represented complete or definite syllables, in which no vowels had to be supplied. The Egyptian syllabic characters differed in another respect from the Assyrian ones. They admitted complementary letters, as they are called; sometimes before them, sometimes after them, and sometimes both before and after them; while the Assyrian characters had no complements. . . .

Dismissing then the idea that the Assyrian mode of writing was in any respect derived from the Egyptians, we have to seek its origin in the lower part of the valley of the Euphrates, where the clayey nature of the soil would account for the plastic character of the writing. The name of Accad occurs in Gen. X, 10, as that of one of the earliest cities in this district, and it is also found in the Assyrian inscriptions, apparently applied to the whole district. It has therefore been chosen with great propriety by Sir H. Rawlinson to represent the people who invented the Assyrian mode of writing. The language of this people may be called Accadian; and there are in existence ample means of attaining to the knowledge of its structure and its vocabulary. The sources of information respecting it are of three sorts. The bilingual tablets in the British Museum were written in the seventh century B.C. Some of these contain Accadian sentences and equivalent Assyrian sentences, either in parallel columns, or one beneath the other. In others, sentences in the two languages are analysed, so as to give the precise meaning of every element in the long Accadian words that we meet. In all the Assyrian inscriptions Accadian words are occasionally introduced; and when different copies of the inscriptions have been found, it often happens that one contains an Accadian word and another its Assyrian equivalent. The oldest Assyrian inscription of considerable length is that of Tiglath Pileser I., whose capital was sacked by the Accadians of Babylon 419 years before the first year of Sennacherib (702 B.C.). The inscription was therefore written a little before 1121 B.C. Inscriptions, the language of which is wholly Accadian and which are anterior to the Assyrian ones, are said to be in existence; but copies of them have not yet been made public. A third source of information as to the glossary of the Accadian language goes back to the origin of this species of writing. The phonetic values of the characters used in the original writing of the Accadians were the names of the objects which the characters represented. We know what certain characters represented, and we know their phonetic values; and thus we come to know the Accadian names of certain objects at the time when this mode of writing was invented. We cannot assign the date of this invention; but we have a minor limit for it. In the inscription of Tiglath Pileser I., who began to reign about 1130 B.C., mention is made of a temple, which after standing 641 years, having become ruinous, had been taken down by the great-grandfather of this king, sixty years before his accession. Sixty is a round number, but is more likely to have been less than greater than the actual number; but the other number which purports to be accurate, was doubtless taken from an authentic record. The temple would therefore have been built about 1830 B.C. Now, Tiglath Pileser found inscriptions written by its builder, who lived before the origin of the Assyrian monarchy; and we have thus the nineteenth century B.C. as the *latest* date at which the origin of Accadian writing can be fixed. Its actual date was in all probability several generations earlier. The bilingual tablets teach us that the Accadian language was in its structure as dissimilar as can well be conceived possible both to the Indo-European languages and to the Semitic ones. It had unmistakeable affinities with the language of the inscriptions found at Susa and in its neighborhood, and with that of the Achaemenian inscriptions of the second kind. These latter had been supposed by Mr. Norris to be connected with the Ugrian languages; while others believed them to be represented by the Mongolian or Dravidian languages. The author, being unacquainted with these languages, declined to express a positive opinion. As respected his arguments in this paper, it was of no consequence whether the Accadian language was represented by one or more living languages, or whether it had died away, like the Egyptian, leaving no representative on the tongues of men. . . .

The Hincks paper of 1857 was sound in some ways but wide

of the mark in others. The consonantal (alphabetic) writing of the Semites and their scribal tradition of writing from right to left were both Syro-Palestinian developments of the second millennium B.C. This was centuries after the cuneiform had begun to be used for writing various Semitic dialects, and thus neither the consonantal writing nor the direction in which it was written was a criterion for determining whether an earlier script had been invented by Semites. On the other hand, Hincks had been quick to see the importance of the new material exploited by Rawlinson and to accept most of the latter's conclusions.

It was in "the bilingual tablets in the British Museum" that Rawlinson had found his new evidence. These were among the thousands of documents written on clay that A. H. Layard, excavating the Assyrian capital of Nineveh, had recently found in the great archives, or library, of Ashurbanipal, the last important Assyrian king. The bilinguals, or "syllabaries," were what might be called the textbooks and reference works used by the Assyrian scribes for the study of Sumerian. By the time of Ashurbanipal in the seventh century B.C. Sumerian had been a dead language for hundreds of years, but like Latin or classical Greek today, it was still studied for religious and cultural purposes.

The "syllabaries" were of various kinds. In one variety, for example, (1) ideographs or pictographs, (2) the corresponding Sumerian words spelled out syllabically, and (3) Assyrian translations were arranged in parallel columns. If we were to follow this practice with our hypothetical English-French system of writing, we might have:

English pronunciation	Character	French word
sē		mer
aye		oeil

In the "syllabaries" in Ashurbanipal's library, Rawlinson found:[5]

SUMERIAN PRONOUNCIATION	CHARACTER	ASSYRIAN WORD	MEANING
GU – U		AL – PU	OX
E		BI – I – TU	HOUSE
A – NA		ŠA – MU – U₂	HEAVEN
DI – IN – GIR₂		I – LUM	GOD
U₂		U₄ – MU	DAY
I – TU		AR – HU	MONTH

---

[5] The decipherers soon discovered that the cuneiform script contained homophones and polyphones. Two *different* characters that have the *same* phonetic value are homophones. A *single* character that has *several different* phonetic values is a polyphone. In the modern system for transliterating the cuneiform the homophones are given subscript numbers. Also, "sh" is transliterated by š. As an illustration of polyphones and homophones:

POLYPHONE	HOMOPHONES
U₄	U
UD	U₂
UT	U₃
TAM	U₄ , ETC.
PAR, ETC.	

There were also paradigms in Sumerian and Assyrian:

MEANING	ASSYRIAN	SUMERIAN
HE PAYS	𒐊 QAL — 𒐊 I - ŠA 𒐊	𒐊 E — 𒐊 LA₂ 𒐊 IN - 𒐊
THEY PAY	𒐊 LU 𒐊 I - ŠA - QA 𒐊	𒐊 NE 𒐊 LA₂ - E 𒐊 IN - 𒐊
HE PAID	𒐊 UL — 𒐊 IŠ - QU₂ 𒐊	𒐊 LA₂ — 𒐊 IN - 𒐊
THEY PAID	𒐊 LU — 𒐊 IŠ - QU₂ 𒐊	𒐊 EŠ — 𒐊 LA₂ 𒐊 IN - 𒐊
HE PAYS HIM	𒐊 ŠU 𒐊 I - ŠA - QAL 𒐊	𒐊 E 𒐊 BA - AN - LA₂ 𒐊 IN - 𒐊
THEY PAY HIM	𒐊 𒐊 I - ŠA - QA₂ - LU - ŠU 𒐊	𒐊 NE 𒐊 BA - AN - LA₂ - E - NE 𒐊 IN - 𒐊

CONTINUED

HE PAID HIM	IŠ – QU₂	UL – ŠU
	IN – BA – AN	LA₂
THEY PAID HIM	IŠ – QU₂ – LU	ŠU
	IN – BA – AN – LA₂	EŠ
HE PLACED	IŠ – KU	UN
	IN	GAR
THEY PLACED	IŠ – KU	—
	IN – GAR – RI	EŠ
HE PLACED HIM	IŠ – KU – UN	ŠU
	IN – BA – AN	GAR
THEY PLACE HIM	I – ŠA – KA – AN – U₂ – ŠU	
	IN – BA – AN – GAR – RI – NE	NE
THEY PLACED HIM	IŠ – KU – NU	ŠU
	IN – BA – AN – GAR – RI	EŠ

Or such lists as:

MEANING	ASSYRIAN	SUMERIAN
FROM HIM	IT - TI - ŠU	KI ... NI ... TA
FROM THEM	IT - TI - ŠU - NU	KI ... NE - NE ... TA
FROM ME	IT - TI - IA	KI ... MU ... TA
FROM US	IT - TI - NI	KI ... ME ... TA
FROM YOU (SINGULAR)	IT - TI - KA	KI ... ZU ... TA
FROM YOU (PLURAL)	IT - TI - KU - NU	KI ... ZU - NE - NE - NE ... TA

The few examples given above show (a) that the two languages differ in vocabulary; (b) that they differ in grammatical structure; and (c) that Sumerian was probably the script for which the cuneiform was originally devised. With regard to grammatical structure, for example, the differences are clear in the position of the pronouns and in the fact that the monosyllabic Sumerian roots *lá* (weigh out= pay) and *gar* (place) do not function at all like the corresponding Semitic verbs from the triliteral roots *šql* (shaqalu) and *škn* (shakanu). We see also that the syllabic value *an* (as in *in-ba-an-lá*) is derived from Sumerian *an(a)*, "heaven."

Rawlinson observed that the structure of the newly discovered language was not like either the Semitic or the Indo-European languages. It seemed most like "Turanian," a name that vaguely applied to a group of languages including Finnish, Hungarian, Turkish, and Mongol. Furthermore, Rawlinson thought that Sumerian resembled the third language (Elamite) of the Bisitun inscription that he had already named "Scythian." This seemed all the more reasonable because the Scythians were believed to be Mongols and were known to have been in the area at one time or another.

Oppert agreed with Hincks and Rawlinson that the cuneiform had not been invented by the Babylonians. Investigating the Sumerian vocabulary, he showed in a brilliant paper that the Sumerians were not native to Mesopotamia nor could they have come from Africa. The proof of this was that the Sumerians lacked names for plants and animals indigenous to those areas. They did not have, for example, a word for "lion," but called lions "big dogs."

Even finding a satisfactory name for the new language discovered in the syllabaries was not easy. Oppert recalled:[6]

> At the beginning of studies on the Assyrian cuneiform, it was generally held without much discussion that the Semitic inhabitants of Mesopotamia had invented the writing in which they

[6] J. Oppert, "Études sumériennes," *Journal Asiatique*, V (1875), pp. 267–321; 442–497. The quotations used here are from pp. 267–268. (Trans. by TBJ).

wrote their language. On the 28th of October 1854, I showed in an article in the *Athenaeum français* that this supposition, regarded as established in fact, could not be entertained. I demonstrated that since the same hieroglyphic characters stood for the same meanings and the same syllables in five different languages, there must have been a single origin of the system [five independent inventions of the same culture trait was simply unthinkable]. Comparison of the words which expressed these meanings excluded the Semites as the inventors [of the system] and pointed in positive fashion to a Turanian origin. What name could be given to this people representing an ancient civilization? I proposed to call the language Kasdo-Scythian, from the Hebrew *Kasdim*: Chaldea. . . . Rawlinson proposed the word Hamitic, which he later changed to Chaldean, or Proto-Chaldean. . . .

In the month of July 1855, I had, just once in my life, the happy experience of meeting Hincks. He rejected, not without reason, the terms Kasdo-Scythian and Chaldean. He proposed the term Akkadian and based it on the following consideration: all the kings of Mesopotamia following their principal title used the subsidiary one of "King of Sumer and Akkad." It therefore seemed probable to him that one of the two people [Sumerians or Akkadians] was the inventor of the writing. He proposed Akkad because the name appeared in the Bible.

The name recommended itself by its easy pronunciation; further, it did not possess the inconvenience of an appellation unknown to everyone. . . .

Later, Oppert himself in 1869 and again in 1872 proposed the name "Sumerian," but it did not gain rapid acceptance. Many people continued to prefer "Akkadian." Oppert complained:[7]

I can say that I have no objection to accepting the term Akkadian if it can be shown to me that it has some merit.

I demand only to see the proof.

I should render to Caesar that which is Caesar's. Hincks' remark seemed reasonable at first, but in examining further the slightly fanciful hypothesis of the Irish scholar, I saw that he

[7] *Ibid.*, pp. 271–272.

had missed the mark. Precisely, if either of the two nations could be regarded as the inventor of cuneiform characters, it should be the Sumerians rather than the Akkadians.

Oppert's arguments in favor of "Sumerian" were not very compelling. Eventually, however, one of the syllabaries gave evidence that the term was indeed applied by the Assyrians and Babylonians to both the people and the language of the inventors of the cuneiform.

* * *

The early attack on the Sumerian Problem had been, as we have seen, almost entirely philological. This approach had yielded spectacular results, but there were questions that could not be answered until archaeologists penetrated the lower levels of the great Mesopotamian mounds where the purely Sumerian remains were to be found. Consequently, when Joseph Halévy, in 1874, began to challenge the conclusions of the philologists, the general harmony that had characterized early progress in Sumerological studies was rudely shattered because Halévy, a vigorous and resourceful debater, could not be beaten down with any of the weapons the philologists then had at hand.

In the *Journal Asiatique* for June 1874, Halévy published the first of many articles that he was to write during the next thirty-five years. His initial paper was entitled "Critical Observations on the Supposed Turanians of Babylonia," and it read as follows:[8]

> For more than twenty years Assyriologists have unanimously assumed that southern Mesopotamia and all of Babylonia were first inhabited by a Turanian population speaking a language belonging to the Ugro-Finnish-Turkish group; that the Turianians, called Akkadians by some, Sumerians by others, had invented the cuneiform system of writing and introduced the Semitic tribes, arriving after them in the same region, to the most indispensable arts of civilized life so that Assyrian-Babylonian civilization was formed by the fusion of two races and two distinct

[8] J. Halévy, "Observations critiques sur les prétendus Touraniens de la Babylonie," *Journal Asiatique*, III (1874), pp. 461–536. The quotations used here are from pp. 461–465; 479; 533–535 (Trans. by TBJ).

groups into a single nationality; later that the Akkadians, identified as Chaldeans by the [classical] authors, constituted a priestly
class which employed their Turanian idiom in magical incantations
and in the most sacred rites of Assyrian-Babylonian religion.

These opinions the Assyriologists deduce from a certain number of documents discovered in the great ruins of Mesopotamia,
documents rendered in Akkadian and sometimes provided with
an interlinear translation in Assyrian.

The evidence of the Akkadian texts has been dogmatically
interpreted. In the numerous group of scholars who are practicing
Assyriologists, the original Turanian character of Babylonian civilization is regarded as a scientifically established fact. . . .

So perfect an agreement among so many scholars does not fail
to be imposing. There is consequently a certain rashness in cast-
ing doubt upon opinions that are considered axiomatic. It is not
without having thought about it a long time that I have decided
to make known my reservations. I first tried to express myself by
communicating directly with the Assyriologists that I have the
honor to count among my friends. In exposing to them frankly
the reasons which hinder me from accepting the Turanian origin
of cuneiform writing, I have never disputed the decipherment
itself of the so-called Akkadian texts; on the contrary, I shall use
the results of decipherment to demonstrate that the texts in
question, far from being written in a Turanian language, are Assyrian texts couched in a special ideographic system which because
of its antiquity was considered to be more sacred than purely phonetic writing. This is why, in my opinion, the Assyrian-Babylonian priests preferred to employ ideographic characters in magic
formulae and incantations which they thought gained in efficacy
through the mystic virtue of the writing.

Verbal communication between my scholarly friends and myself with regard to the origin of the cuneiform has not led to any
change in our respective convictions. Each of us persists in his
original opinion. . . .

Finally, Halévy decided to appeal to a larger audience:

The subject that I propose to examine can be summarized in
three questions:

1. Does the Akkadian language, assuming that it exists, belong to the Turanian family?

2. Can one assume the existence of a Turanian people on the soil of Babylonia?

3. Do the texts called Akkadian use a language different from Assyrian, or simply constitute an ideographic system invented by the Assyrians themselves in addition to phonetic writing?

Halévy then went on to show that from the phonetic point of view the so-called Akkadian did not resemble Turanian. This was true, since it was only in grammatical form that a similarity could be seen or sensed.

Next he said:

The existence of a civilized people, caused by the vicissitudes of history to disappear from its native soil, reveals itself to posterity in four different ways:

1. By the monuments which it has left;

2. By the geographic names derived from the language which it spoke;

3. and 4. By the testimony of literary sources or by local tradition.

Yet, said Halévy, there was nothing known in Babylonian art that suggested two different artistic traditions likely to have been left by the Turanians on the one hand and the Babylonians on the other. Moreover, no geographic names of Turanian origin could be discovered, and the ancient authors knew only the Chaldeans, a people of obviously Semitic character. He attacked the theory that the phrase "King of Sumer and Akkad" was evidence that two different groups, the Sumerians and Akkadians, lived in Babylonia. The phrase was always rendered in the same order, "Sumer and Akkad," and if the Akkadians were Semites, as some scholars had claimed, why did not known Semitic kings change the order to "Akkad and Sumer"? Still further, the ancient classical writers consistently gave credit to the Babylonians for the invention of writing; there was no contrary tradition relating to this subject.

He concluded as follows:

It seems to have been established:

1. That Akkadian phonetics differ absolutely from those which distinguish the Ural-Altaic languages;

2. That the grammar of the Turanians on the one hand and that of the Akkadians on the other are diametrically opposed;

3. That there does not exist any reasonable similarity between the Akkadian vocabulary and that which belongs to the Ugro-Finnish languages.

After recapitulating his arguments about the single art tradition, the absence of suggestive geographic names, the evidence of the classical authors, and the like, he said:

The composition and the use of cuneiform signs in the so-called Akkadian documents show them to be characters belonging to an artificial system....

The totality of these results permit us to conclude that the theory which attributes to the Turanians the invention of cuneiform writing and the origin of Babylonian-Assyrian civilization is a gratuitous hypothesis which is not without danger for the progress of historical studies relating to Hither Asia.

Halévy did not make many converts: there were a few, but some of those apostatized later. What Halévy did accomplish was to set off a long series of debates in which he fought almost single-handedly against a formidable array of scholars. Reason and impartiality became more and more rare as the struggle progressed. Bitter personal invective was exchanged that did nothing to settle the question under debate. The remarks that Oppert and Halévy addressed to one another in 1889 provide a representative sample:[9]

STATEMENT OF M. JULES OPPERT

For fifteen years M. Halévy has maintained against all the Assyriologists an inadmissible thesis which has not received the ac-

---

[9] J. Oppert and J. Halévy in "Correspondance," *Revue des études juives*, XVIII (1889), pp. 142–147 (Trans. by TBJ).

ceptance of the scholarly world. In spite of the most irrefutable proof, Halévy will not admit that anyone but the Semites invented cuneiform writing and that the ancient inhabitants of Mesopotamia used a language foreign to the Semitic family. There is more: inscriptions written in two different languages with the same system of writing are regarded by him as two ways of writing the same language. The first conceals the pronunciation by rebus-writing; it is a kind of cryptography or allography expressing "a language of the gods and spirits." The second, with regard to the first, gives the true pronunciation in Assyrian. But why should they write the same text one time to conceal it and another time to make it known? For fifteen years this question has been asked of Halévy, and for fifteen years he has refused to reply. If we were to take the *Phèdre* of Racine and the German translation of it by Schiller, we should have to reason as follows according to the precepts of Halévy: there is a tragedy, *Phèdre*, written cryptographically by Racine and another time written plainly by Schiller. *We* would ordinarily think that the text of Racine was an original written in French by Racine and then translated into German by Schiller. But this is wrong! The supposed French tragedy never existed. It is a rebus version of the text of Schiller, and *Phèdre* is nothing but a German play. If Assyriology were a discipline less new and its findings less subject to debate, this theory [of Halévy] would not survive for long, but what is not possible elsewhere *can* happen in Assyriology because of the newness of the study and the incredulity with which the general public regards it.

But Sayce, Lenormant, Schrader, and I have shown in voluminous writings the correctness of the point of view that we hold regarding the non-Semitic origin of cuneiform writing and on the non-Semitic language that is represented in various cuneiform texts, and we have convinced all competent scholars that we are on the right track. Without mentioning Hincks, Rawlinson, Norris, Birch, Cox, Talbot, Sayce, Lenormant, and Schrader, we can cite George Smith, Coxe, Vaux, Layard, Rassam, Haughton, Pinches, Budge, Boll, Father Strassmaier, the learned editor of so many texts, Evetts, Lyon, and others in England, Haupt, Hommel, Jenson, Lehman, Bezold, and the whole German school; Ménant,

Amiaud, Heuzey, Ledrain, Quentin, Révillout, Babelon, Grébaut, Maspéro, in France; Oberzinner, Krall and others in Austria; Finozi in Italy, and finally other scholars in Russia, Spain, and America. All those who know the subject refuse to be associated with the ideas of M. Halévy.

On the particular topic which has been treated by Halévy in Vol. 33 of this *Revue*—the identity of Hammurabi and Amraphel, who were not contemporaneous but separated from each other by many centuries—I refer the reader to my proof set forth in the *Compte rendu de l'Académié des Inscriptions et Belles-Lettres*. I am not going to go over the whole matter again, but I shall deal only with the errors which Halévy attributes to me. I have never said that the Arioch of the Bible was the son of Kedor-laomer—the latter does not appear in cuneiform texts at all. Halévy thinks that Kedorlaomer is identical with Kudurmabug who appears in the texts as the father of another and later Arioch. Accepting this theory as proven, he goes on to criticize me on other grounds. I do not accept the validity of the arguments hurled against me with regard to the Elamite language since if it were not for my discoveries no one would know anything about it.

To sum up, Halévy has never replied to the arguments advanced in opposition to his thesis. It is radically false, but in a discipline so new which gives rise to so many disagreements, the public is easily misled, and I think that it is my duty to try to clarify matters. This is the only excuse I have for not keeping silent.

RESPONSE OF M. HALÉVY

M. Oppert is one of the scholars who has created the Sumerian theory. It is perfectly legitimate that he should believe in the existence of the Sumerian language and the non-Semitic origin of cuneiform writing, but I demand the right and the liberty to maintain an opposing opinion on these matters, one that I have scientifically sustained. I am ready to recant when convicted of error, but no one has brought forward against me a scientific argument. I cannot bow before authoritarian pronouncements or lists which prove that the old theory had a large number of supporters. My learned adversary is not so much interested in the question which divides us as he is imposing the acceptance of his authority, and the alleged multitude of his supporters can be cut down to practically nothing. Among the thirty-eight scholars listed by him as judges who condemn my theory, four were dead before my opposition had seen the light of day: these are Hincks, Norris, Layard, and Finzi; seven others—Birch, Cox, Vaux, Heuzy, Babelon, Grébaut, Maspero—are specialists in archaeology or Egyptology who have never occupied themselves with Sumerian linguistics. The same thing can be said with regard to Rassam, Haughton, Oberzinner, and Krall whose work on this subject is not known to me. As for the rest who may properly be called Assyriologists . . . three-fourths have never published [on this particular subject]. The only ones who have made even tentative efforts are Schrader, Sayce, Haupt, and the deceased Lenormant. Oppert himself published only a little note—and that was ten years ago. Facing these five pro-Sumerians, the anti-Sumerians can bring up three defenders: the late Stanislas Guyard, Professor Friedrich Delitzsch, and my humble self. Where then is this solid front of competent scholars who condemn my theory? Evidently the expression is a little hyperbolic.

If I have insisted that Babylonian cuneiform is Semitic, it is not because of considerations of race, but solely because the cuneiform shows the phonetic traits of the Semitic languages. I have never discussed the basic aptitudes of races. I have never said that other people did not have the capacity necessary to invent writing of this kind.

I have not said that the system which I call hieratic is a crytography that conceals the pronunciation by means of rebus. I have protested against this allegation many times. In place of "conceal," the rebus "recalls" and "indicates" the word which is "expressed," sometimes imperfectly . . . The essence of the system is always the "suggestion" of the word, not its "concealment."

The simultaneous use of two systems, hieratic and phonetic, by the Babylonians has its parallel in our use of Roman and Arabic numerals side by side with numbers expressed by letters. . . . To compare the anti-Sumerians to those who would consider the

Phèdre of Racine as a cryptographic form of the *Phèdre* by Schiller is an easy way to polemicize. Nothing would be easier than for me to make fun of my opponents in the same manner. They have invented the Sumerian people who never existed, and they have attributed to them a language which was never spoken. You can imagine the clever remarks I could make on that subject.

I have never said, as Oppert alleges, that the Arioch of Genesis was the son of Amraphel, and I do not know where Oppert got the idea that I attributed this opinion to him. As for the date of Hammurabi, which would be two centuries before that of Abraham, I shall be willing to accept that when someone can prove it; but at present no proof has been given.

If the reading of scientific works carries the right to call oneself the pupil of their authors, then I gladly declare myself the pupil of all Assyriologists. Likewise, I shall learn from future works about things that I do not know now. I stand ready to make reply in the periodicals devoted to such questions with regard to all arguments by which anyone cares to oppose me; and also on special questions, as in this *Revue*, in which I have been in disagreement with Oppert. To reasoned arguments, one responds with reasoned arguments, and not with pronouncements.

COUNTER-REPLY OF M. OPPERT

The arguments of Halévy relieve me of any responsibility for a reply. The *Phèdre* of Racine, according to Halévy, does not "conceal" the German *Phèdre*. It "suggests" and "indicates" it in rebus form which is composed of "ideographs and phonograms." I did not choose this example jokingly, but rather because it exactly represents Halévy's theory. Let us take now the example of a king who spent his money to have engraved on a hard stone a long inscription in two parallel columns, which began thus:

First Column	*Second Column*
Ha-am-mu-ra-bi	Ha-am-mu-ra-bi
lugal kalagga	šarru dannu
ur-sag	qar-ra-du

As an illustration of a bilingual text, we have included here (Figure 1) a portion of an inscription of Sargon of Akkad.

These two texts are: one, Sumerian; the other, Assyrian. They say exactly the same thing, each in its own language. We give a French translation in a third column:

Hammurabi,
the mighty king,
the hero

As for the proper name (of Hammurabi) one is astonished that
it should not "suggest" or indicate by a "rebus," an "ideogram," or
a "phonogram."

Who now wishes to contend, by applying the theory of
Halévy, that the first and second columns are crytographic and
should be pronounced exactly like the text of column three? The
first and second columns are only concealed French! I have already said that for fifteen years, Halévy has maintained his thesis
without having made any serious converts. He criticizes me because some of the scholars whom I have named as partisans of my
opinions were dead before having an opportunity to read his
arguments, but they were nevertheless convinced while living of
the existence of Sumerian. It was Hincks who invented the word
Akkadian to describe the language of which Halévy denies the
existence. Norris often used the word. So did Finzi. Layard is
still alive, and the eminent scholars that Halévy would brush aside
have a competence equal to his, and they unanimously condemn
his point of view.

All the arguments of Halévy collapse as easily as those to which
I have replied. I am not "one of the inventors," but rather "the
inventor" of Sumerian. Today many young scholars are engaged
in studying the grammar of that language. . . .

I have never seen a table of logarithms written in two columns,
one in Roman characters and the other in Arabic.

The date of Hammurabi is chronologically established. I regret that I cannot furnish Halévy with a mathematical demonstration of this, but it is not possible for me to project myself
into the nether world.

The scientific proofs against Halévy do not convince him. He
ought to bear in mind that no one ever has the last word. We
cannot avoid the fact that others will come after us. They will
render the final decision.

Three years later, in 1892, Christopher Johnston of the John Hopkins University read a paper at the April meeting of the American Oriental Society. Describing what was then the current state of the Sumerian Problem, Johnston said:[10]

At a comparatively early period in the history of Assyriology it became evident to investigators that the cuneiform tablets of Assyria and Babylonia presented not only a Semitic language, but also, alongside of it, an idiom differing widely from the Semitic type both in grammar and in vocabulary. A peculiar feature of this latter idiom was the fact that it was written for the most part in ideograms, with which were combined certain phonetic elements, serving to indicate the proper pronunciation of words and to constitute grammatical forms. In structure it bore some resemblance to the so-called Turanian group, and at all events was distinctly agglutinative. The numerous texts composed in it were, with exception of the inscriptions of some early Babylonian kings, almost exclusively of a religious character, consisting of hymns, penitential psalms, charms, exorcisms, and magical formulae of various sorts, usually accompanied by an interlinear or parallel Semetic version. It was further found that the old Assyrian and Babylonian scholars had devoted much attention to the study of this language, and had composed a considerable number of lexicographical and grammatical works for its elucidation.

This non-Semitic idiom received from the earlier Assyriologists various names—Sumerian, Akkadian, Proto-Babylonian, Proto-Chaldean—and was regarded by them as the speech of a people who preceded the Semites in Babylonia, invented the cuneiform system of writing, and laid the foundations of Babylonian civilization. From this ancient people, it was believed, the Semitic immigrants or invaders derived their civilization, and in large measure also their religious conceptions; so that when, in course of time, the Semite element of the population and the Semitic language became predominant, the old tongue was preserved as a ritual language, holding the same place that Latin holds to-day in the Roman Catholic church. This would explain the fact that the

[10] C. Johnston, "The Sumero-Accadian Question," *Journal of the American Oriental Society*, XV (1893), pp. 317–322.

great majority of the non-Semitic texts are of a religious nature, as also the zeal of the Assyro-Babylonian priestly scholars in its study and preservation. Such, down to the year 1874, was the general opinion on the subject; the only materal points respecting which scholars were at all at variance was the minor one of nomenclature.

In 1874, however, the distinguished French epigraphist Joseph Halévy propounded a novel theory, which he has since defended with great ability. According to him, the so-called Akkadian or Sumerian people are a pure myth; no such people ever existed. The Semites were the real inventors of cuneiform writing, which, originally ideographic, was in course of time developed into a phonetic system, just as is the case with Egyptian. The priests, however, in order to lend an air of greater mystery to their sacred writings and render them incomprehensible to the profane vulgar, devised a most ingenious and complicated system of cryptography. Taking the old Semitic ideograms as its basis, they assigned to them conventional phonetic values and meanings, and, adding to them certain arbitrarily chosen signs to represent pronouns, particles, and grammatical forms, they invented, not a new language, but a mysterious allographic method of writing the Semitic Assyro-Babylonian. The priestly method Halévy styles Hieratic, the ordinary method Demotic. These views were earnestly combatted by the upholders of the older theory, and, though the question has been vigorously debated down to the present time, the battle is still in progress.

In 1880 a new feature was introduced into the controversy by the discovery that the non-Semitic language appeared in two different forms, each possessing certain peculiarities; that one of these forms was the language of the hymns and penitential psalms, and the other that of the incantations; and that this difference had been recognized by the old Assyrian priestly scholars, who had drawn up special vocabularies for the explanation of the two forms, to one of which, the idiom of the penitential psalms, they applied the technical designation of *eme sal*, generally translated "female (or woman's) language." At first the difference was regarded as dialectic, some Assyriologists holding that the *eme sal* was the dialect of Sumer or Southern Babylonia, and that the incantations were composed in that of Akkad or in Northern-Babylonian, while others held that the incantations were South-Babylonian or Sumerian, and the penitential psalms North-Baby-lonian or Akkadian. Later, however, the theory was introduced that the difference was not local but temporal; that the idiom of the incantations was the older, and should be styled Old Sumerian or simply Sumerian; and that the penitential psalms presented a later form of the language of the incantations, to be designated as Neo-Sumerian.

To sum up the whole question in a few words, the Sumerists hold that Sumerian was a real language, spoken by the primitive inhabitants of Babylonia, and appearing in two forms differing from each other either locally or temporally; while the position of J. Halévy and other anti-Sumerists, whose ranks have been strengthened by such distinguished scholars as the late Stanislas Guyard of Paris and Prof. Friedrich Delitzsch of Leipzig, is that it was no language at all, but merely a figment of the priestly class, a pure cryptography.

It is obviously beyond the scope of a brief paper like this to attempt to decide a question which has been debated by able scholars for many years. It may, however, be allowable to present some of the principal arguments on each side, and to offer some considerations as to the manner in which the question must finally be decided.

The chief arguments brought forward by the anti-Sumerists against the existence of a Sumerian language and in favor of the Semitic origin of cuneiform writing are as follows:

1. If, they say, such a people really existed, and played such an important part in the civilization of the Semites, why are they never mentioned in the cuneiform inscriptions? Why have they left no memorials of themselves in the shape of temples, sculptures, or inscriptions?

2. We find that a considerable number of the phonetic values of cuneiform characters are indubitably of Semitic origin, being derived from the initial syllables of the Semitic words they ideographically represent. To illustrate this by a few examples: The characters which, as phonograms, have the values of *is*, *bit ša*,

dan, *sab*, are identical with the characters which, as ideograms, represent respectively the Semitic words *isu* "wood," *bîtu*, "house," *šakânu* "make," *dannu* "mighty," and *sâbu* "soldier." Nor does this occur in only a few cases, or even in comparatively few cases; it is true in a considerable number of instances. If then we could trace back to its source every phonetic value, it is more reasonable, they say, to infer that all would be found to proceed from a Semitic origin than to assume a derivation from another idiom.

3. The so-called Sumerian contains such a large proportion of genuine, although more or less thinly disguised, Semitic words as to exclude the idea of simple borrowing. The theory of the existence of Sumerian therefore falls to the ground, since the remaining words which cannot now be referred to Semitic roots, either in Assyrian or in the cognate languages, may really be good Semitic words from obsolete roots, or may be purely conventional words invented by the priests.

4. In the matter of grammar, Sumerian, it is claimed, presents many points of contact with Assyrian. It possesses a *šu* stem and a *ta-an* stem, corresponding with the Assyrian *šafel* and stems with infixed *t;* its adverbial ending is *eš*, corresponding to the Assyrian adverbial ending *iš;* Sumerian *'ge*, like Assyrian *lû*, is not only a precative but an emphatic particle, and moreover *'ge-a . . . 'ge'a,* like *lû . . . lû*, means "whether . . . or"; Sumerian, like Assyrian, has suffix pronouns. The inference is plain that such forms can only be due to a conscious imitation of Semitic grammar. Such briefly are the principal arguments on which the anti-Sumerists rest their case.

The Sumerists answer as follows:

1. Even if it were true that the Sumerians are never mentioned and that they have left no traces, nothing would be proved thereby. Babylonia has been as yet only partially explored, and ample memorials of this people may come to light at any day. But it is not true. The Sumerians are mentioned in the cuneiform texts, and there are numerous traces of them in Babylonia. If Hammurabi had bilingual inscriptions composed in Semitic and Sumerian, it was certainly not with the view of concealing their

meaning. The statues found at Tel-Loh by M. de Sarzec are decidedly not of a Semitic type, and can only be regarded as memorials of the ancient Sumerians.

That many characters possess Semitic phonetic values is precisely what we might expect. No one can suppose that the Semites simply appropriated the Sumerian system of writing without any modification. They must necessarily have adapted it to the needs of their language and its phonetic system. That in the process of adaptation new phonetic values were introduced, and these too derived from the Semitic values of the ideograms, was most natural. Moreover, almost invariably the Sumerian phonetic value was retained alongside of the Semitic. Taking the examples cited above, we have:

> is, Ass. *iṣu;* but Sum. *giš* = "wood"
> bit, Ass. *bîtu;* but Sum. *ê* = "house"
> ša, Ass. *šakânu;* but Sum. *gar* = "make"
> dan, Ass. *dannu;* but Sum. *kala* = "mighty"
> ṣab, Ass. *ṣâbu;* but Sum. *erim* = "soldier"

That many Semitic words are to be found in Sumerian is an undoubted fact; but their number is greatly less than is claimed by the anti-Sumerists. It is acknowledged by all that nearly all the Sumerian texts we possess may have been composed, long after the language had ceased to be spoken, by priestly scholars who acquired it as a learned accomplishment, and that, just as in the case of mediaeval Latin, many foreign words would naturally creep in. But the anti-Sumerists have been led to extremes by the craze for Semitic etymologies, and have made many palpable errors.

2. As regards the grammar, the resemblance is merely superficial. The *šu* and *ta-an* stems by no means coincide with the Assyrian *šafel* and stems with infixed *t*. Many languages possess suffix-prepositions. The other resemblances are either accidental or due to the Semitic environments of the scribes. To offset these superficial resemblances, there remains the fact that the whole structure of Akkadian grammar is radically different from that of Assyrian.

This, then, is the position of the Sumerists, and they do little more than attempt to refute the arguments of their opponents. In fact, the whole treatment of the question by both sides is far from satisfactory. The anti-Sumerists seek to draw deductions from a number of isolated examples, and from the inherent probabilities of the case. The Sumerists, as a rule, assuming the correctness of their views, throw the burden of proof upon their adversaries, and content themselves with refuting the arguments they advance. Something more than this is necessary. Dr. Lehmann, it is true, in his *Samuššumukîn* (which has recently appeared), seems to recognize this, and devotes considerable space to establishing the fact that Sumerian possesses a definite phonetic and syntactic system, radically different from the Assyrian. Even this is not sufficient, as such conditions are by no means incompatible with the theory of artificiality.

The arguments outlined above are useful as corroborative testimony, but they do not go down to the root of the matter.

The question can only be decided on the basis of the idiom itself. If Sumerian was ever a living language, it must present the phenomena of a living language. If it does this, no amount of loan-words, however large, can invalidate its claim to a real existence. Modern Persian has borrowed so freely from Arabic as to give rise to the saying that any good Arabic word is a good Persian word; yet it will never be considered a Semitic language. The question then resolves itself into this: does Sumerian present those organic phenomena which are characteristic of living speech?

1. As to its phonology—Do we find instances of assimilation, dissimilation, vowel-harmony, or other changes dependent on the adjacent sounds?

2. As to its vocabulary—Do the Sumerian words present characteristic concepts? Or, as it must be studied through the medium of Assyrian, the question can be put in another form: are the same Sumerian words invariably rendered by the same Assyrian words in the way of a mere slavish reproduction? Or are they rendered by different words, according to the shade of meaning to be expressed, so that they clearly represent individually concepts peculiar to their idiom? In other words, are there

such differences of rendering as always occur in translating—say from German into English?

3. As to the forms—Do the same Sumerian always correspond to the same Assyrian grammatical forms? Or do we find such differences as may justly be considered due to a difference in the organization of the two languages? For example, do we find cases in which the same Sumerian verb-forms are variously rendered in Assyrian, and vice versa?

4. As to the syntax—Is the Sumerian sentence merely modeled on the Assyrian? or does it possess characteristics which can find their analogy in any living speech?

5. How far does Semitism on the part of the scribe enter into cases of resemblance? and, on the other hand, to what extent does the Sumerian influence Assyrian translation?

It is on these lines, and these alone, that the question can be definitely settled. The whole bilingual literature must be carefully gone over, and all instances bearing on the above points collected. The mass of material thus gathered must be thoroughly sifted, and all doubtful cases eliminated. When this work is done, and the results have been tabulated and studied, we shall be in a position to draw our conclusions with the least possibility of error, and to settle definitely the much vexed Sumero-Akkadian question.

Eight years later the argument was still raging. Theophilus G. Pinches, a British scholar, published a long article in the *Journal of The Royal Asiatic Society* for 1900. This article is given below with the exception of Pinches' highly technical linguistic examples, which have been deleted.[11]

Fifteen years ago I read before this Society a paper treating of "the languages of the Early Inhabitants of Mesopotamia," in which I expressed my conviction that the non-Semitic dialects (for there are at least two closely-allied idioms) spoken in that district, revealed to us by the Babylonian and Assyrian inscrip-

[11] T. G. Pinches, "Sumerian or Cryptography," *Journal of the Royal Asiatic Society*, XXXII (1900), pp. 75–96. The quotations used here are taken from pp. 75–79; 94–95.

tions, were really languages, and not cryptographies or "allographic systems of writing," as they were called by those who favoured the theory of the artificial nature of the script employed.

At that time, as nearly as I can recollect, there were but two Assyriologists who held the theory to which I have referred, namely, Halévy, who first put it forth, and Guyard, who was, I believe, one of his pupils. Later on, Fried. Delitzsch joined the band, but afterwards recanted his heresy on seeing how many difficulties attended the acceptance of the explanations offered. Of late years, however, in the increasing ranks of the Assyriologists, M. Halévy has found several supporters, and the time has come to turn attention to this theory that has been advanced, and which has gained in importance with those who do not know, and who naturally think that, as the hypothesis put forward has now many adherents, there is at least great probability that those who hold the older opinion are wrong.

At this point, however, I should like clearly to define the ground that I shall cover in the present paper. What I should like to do would be, to go over all the arguments that have been advanced in favour of the theory that those ancient idioms of the Mesopotamian plains were not languages, but "allographies," and examine dispassionately and carefully each one, quoting all the points for and against, and drawing a conclusion from an examination of the whole. This, unfortunately, I am unable to do for want of time; the examination of the many papers that have been written by M. Halévy alone would have bespoken my leisure hours for many weeks, and rendered the writing of this paper impossible.

A few words upon the arguments advanced are necessary, however, to make the reader understand the nature of the question at issue, and this is probably best done by describing what the documents are with which students of Assyrian have to deal.

The most important of the inscriptions of Babylonia and Assyria for the language in general are the bilingual texts, which give mainly hymns to the gods, incantations, psalms of a penitential nature, etc., with a few historical texts. These inscriptions are generally interlinear, but are sometimes written in parallel col-

umns, *the non-Semitic version being always first.* As in the case of
the Assyrian inscriptions in general, however, these documents
would of themselves be of but little value without the syllabaries,
which give us the various pronunciations of the syllables of
which the words and groups are composed.

These syllabaries are of various kinds. The simplest are those
giving the pronunciation, the character, and the name of the
character. A second class gives the pronunciation, the character,
and its meaning when so pronounced in the non-Semitic idiom. A
third class gives the pronunciation, the character or group, the
name or names of the character or group, and the meaning in
Assyrian. Yet another class gives a list of non-Semitic words
pronounced (or written) in the same way when phonetically
rendered, the characters by which they are expressed when
ideographically written, and their meanings. In addition to these
important documents bearing on the pronunciation of the non-
Semitic idiom (the so-called system of rebuses), there is a large
number of bilingual lists with non-Semitic (Sumerian) glosses, and
at least one fragment exists of a narrative text written in three
lines (not columns), giving (first) the non-Semitic words of the
inscription, (second) the pronunciation of the words in the first
line, and (third) the meaning in Assyrian.

If we take a portion of a syllabary of the first series, that with
the values of the character and its name or names, we shall find
that the names of the characters are formed from the values.
Thus the value of the character meaning "great" is *gal*, a syllable
which, in the non-Semitic idiom, has the same meaning. By at-
taching to the syllable *gal* the Assyrian nominative ending *u*,
and doubling the *l*, we get the form *gallu*, the name of the character, which is sometimes used (and then it is not, naturally, the
name of the character) in Assyrian as a synonym of the Semitic
word *rabû*, meaning "great." Other examples of this are *hullu*,
from *hul*, "evil"; *mahhu*, from *mah*, "supreme"; *mâšu*, from *mâš*,
"double"; *dimmu*, from *dim*, "cord"; *ênu*, from *ên*, "lord"; *tappu*,
from *tab*, "companion"; *êdinu*, from *êdin*, "plain" ("Eden"); *te-
mennu*, from *temena*, "memorial-cylinder"; *dû*, from *dû*, "seat,
mound"; with many others.

Besides these, however, a number of words, evidently borrowed, are common to both idioms, both Assyrian and non-Semitic. Thus we have *ê-gala* and *êkallu*, 'great house' or "palace"; *dup-sara* and *dupšarru*, "scribe"; *gala* and *gallu*, "demon, devil"; *namtara* and *namtaru*, "fate"; *sa-bara* and *saparu*, "net"; *ušbar* and *ušparu*, "loom"; *guza* and *kussû*, "throne"; *mada* and *mâtu*, "land, country"; *ḫarran* and *ḫarranu*, "road"; *abzu* and *apsû*, "abyss"; *ibila* and *ablu*, "son"; *duba* and *duppu*, "tablet"; *saga* and *saku*, head, end" (of a piece of ground); *bala* and *palû*, "regnal year"; *lamma* and *lamassu*, "colossus"; *banšur* and *paššuru*, "dish"; *sah* and *sahu*, "pig"; *adama* and *adamatu*, "gore, blood"; *isaga* (*nisaga*) and *iššaku*, (*nisakku*), "prince, chief"; *umbin* and *ubanu* "finger"; *nun* and *nûnu*, "fish"; *urudu* and *éru*, "copper"; *illat* or *ellat*, "army"; *urugala*, *arali*, and *arallu*, "hades"; *sangu* and *šangû*, "priest" (both from *sag*, "head"!); *sukkal* and *sukkalu*, "messenger"; *agarin* and *agarinnu*, "mother"; *kisal* and *kisallu*, "platform"; *ušumgal* and *ušumgallu*, "peerless one, demon"; *bara* and *parakku*, "shrine"; *silim* and *salimu* or *šulmu*, "peace"; *nér*, the *neros* (600); *damgar* and *tamkaru*, "agent"; *ingar* and *igaru*, "enclosure"; *gidim* and *êdimmu*, *utug* and *utukku*, names of evil spirits; *egâ* and *agû*, "inundation," with many others.

Some of my readers will probably have recognized, in this list of similar words in the two idioms, a few roots that are common Semitic property. *Êkallu* is, of course, the common word *hēkāl*, "temple"; *dupšarru* is the Hebrew *tipsar*, used in Jeremiah and Nahum for "governor"; *kussū* is the well-known word for "throne," in Heb. *kissē* and in Arabic *kursî*; *nunu*, "fish"; *silim*, *šulmu*, and *salīmu*, "peace"; and others which are not so easy to identify on account of the transformations they have undergone, but whose derivations have been worked out, and are known, may also be noted. Among these are *ḫarranu*, "road," from *ḫararu*, "to make a furrow"; *ibila* and *âblu*, "son," from *âbalu*, "to produce"; *adama* and *adamatu*, "blood" or "gore," from the same root as Adam, Edom, etc.; *illat* or *ellat*, "army," the Heb. *ḫeyil* or *ḫēl*, "army, fortification," whilst *damgar* and *tamkaru*, "agent," are connected with the word *makkuru*, "property."

When two nationalities come together, or have close communication with each other, it is the usual thing for an interchange of words to take place, for it is certain that they will both possess expressions or meanings of synonymous words wanting to one or the other, and this being the case, they will be under the necessity of borrowing unless the needful synonym can be coined easily. This, however, seldom happens, and they borrow, often (as in the case of our own language) when there is little or no need for it, for after a time words become commonplace, "worn out," so to say, and foreign words take their place even though good words expressing the same ideas already exist. This is the true explanation of the fact that the Semitic and non-Semitic idioms of ancient Mesopotamia have so much in common.

One of the most interesting arguments against the theory that the non-Semitic idiom of Babylonia is an allography or something of the sort, however, is its difference gramatically from the Semitic idiom spoken in the country. Many of the phrases that we find in the bilingual texts are, of course, straightforward enough, and present no difficulty. Take, for instance, the following:

Sumerian:	*Ene*	*gae*	*munšin-gen*
Assyro-Bab.:	*Bêlum*	*yâti*	*išpuranni*
	"The lord,	as for me,	he sent to me."

Here the word-order is the same in both the non-Semitic and the Semitic idioms, but even in this case it is to be noted that the root of *munšingen* is *gen*, and that the rest of the word consists wholly of particles added to the root to make the meaning more precise, and repeating, practically, the pronouns. Thus the first component, *mun*, means "me," *si* means "to," and *in* means "he," the full signification of the verb being "me to he sent," whilst the Semitic Babylonian verbal form with the pronoun *išpuranni*, is to be analyzed *išpur*, "he sent," and *(a)nni*, "me" or "to me." The non-Semitic idiom is, therefore, the more precise of the two, and shows, even in this simple phrase, a noteworthy departure from the Semitic idiom.

But much more striking differences than this are to be found.

So strong was the tendency in the non-Semitic idiom to throw particles to the end of a clause, that we even find them placed after the verb at the conclusion of the phrase instead of being at the beginning, as in Semitic Babylonian, where, according to the rules of grammar, they ought to be.

Sumerian:	*Kurkurra*	*ama*	*banda*	*bada-*
	In the mountains	wild bull	mighty	in it
	nâ	*qime.*		
	lying down	like.		

According to the Semitic translation, however, this is to be rendered as follows:

Ina šadâni kima rêmi îodi rabšu, "He lies down in the mountains like a mighty wild bull," from which it may be gathered that the word *qime* in the non-Semitic line ought to come either after *ama,* "wild bull," or after *banda,* "mighty." In all probability this word-order is due to poetical form, especially as it is found in three successive lines, but as it is against all the rules of Assyrian grammar, and unusual even in the non-Semitic idiom, this is surely an argument against the theory that the latter is a mere invention of the Semitic population of the country.

To sum up:

1. There are numerous tablets written in a non-Semitic dialect, with and without translation into Semitic Babylonian, and in two cases at least these non-Semitic texts are expressly designated as Sumerian.

2. That Sumerian (or Akkadian) was not an allography is proved by the fact that it possessed a dialect showing clear laws of sound-change. It is to be noted also that the grammar is entirely different from that of the Semitic idiom.

3. The type of the earliest monuments is distinctly different from that of the later period, when the Semites gained the ascendency; and also different from the type exhibited by the comparatively ancient kingdom of Agadé, where, notwithstanding, non-Semitic influence must, before the time of Sargon (Sargani) of Agadé, have been sufficiently strong to leave at least some impress.

4. The language of the inscriptions which often accompany the type exhibited by the above-named earliest monuments is al-

ways non-Semitic, and must, as such, be regarded as the language of the people represented.

5. Not only hymns, psalms, incantations, charms, and similar literary products were written in the non-Semitic language to which I have referred, but also royal inscriptions, legal precepts, and law documents, the latter classes of texts being such as no sane person would write in any so-called "allography." All these classes of documents were later, when Semitic civilization became general, composed in the Semitic Babylonian language, and this fact alone ought to do away with any doubt as to the nationality of the pioneers of civilization in the Euphrates Valley.

Halévy responded to Pinches and to others of his critics, but his blows had lost their power and his aim was frequently so poor that he landed wide of the target. He had shot his bolt, but we may take one last look at the shining knight whom the passing years had transformed into a pitiable Don Quixote:[12]

I should like to sketch a rustic parable which concludes, I regret to say, in the manner of Matthew XXV, 24.

Three farmers went out to thresh a large field full of magnificent grain. . . . After the first hour they were joined by other workers. On sorting out the wheat, they discovered two species, one more variegated than the other. The threshers sold the variegated species at a high price under the name of Far Eastern wheat alleging that it had been crossed with grain from the Amour River imported by prehistoric Mongols. One of the laborers, however, decided to submit the two species to a chemical analysis and found that the apparent difference between the two varieties was due to accidental causes for which the local climate was responsible. The others called this blasphemous, and, in order to make an example, forced one of the best workers who had accepted the results of the chemical analysis to retract his statements. Nevertheless, the sellers of wheat became aware of the danger of having to prove the quality of their merchandise, and many of them sought other occupations. The price of the

[12] J. Halévy, "C. P. Tiele et la question sumérienne," *Journal Asiatique*, VIII (1900), pp. 9–22. The quotations used here are taken from pp. 9–10. (Trans. by TBJ).

variegated wheat fell off considerably, but then came the workers of the second hour: in their hands the pen had replaced the pick of the laborer, the sickle of the reaper, and the sieve of the thresher. They not only registered the grain for the agricultural census, but also they took care to restore to first place the discredited name of Far Eastern wheat.

And here is the meaning:

The productive field is Assyriology; the threshers are Rawlinson, Hincks, and Oppert; the workers are the Assyriologists who have contributed to the decipherment and the explication of the texts; the ordinary grains of wheat are the Semitic texts, the variegated grains—the "Sumerian" texts; the label "Far Eastern," Sumerianism. The result of the chemical analysis is "anti-Sumerianism," and the worker of the second hour who thought of the test is a well-known Assyriologist. The census officials of the last hour who, to use the words of the Evangelist (Matthew XXV, 25), "reap where they have not sowed and gather where they have not winnowed," are the general historians who pretend that they have the ability to settle difficult and infinitely complicated questions that baffle the specialists in the field.

This was the end of an era. Halévy was discredited. General historians of antiquity, like Eduard Meyer, or those who assayed to synthesize what had been learned about "Babylonian civilization," like Jastrow, had accepted the views of the Sumerianists. As Oppert had warned: "They, the next generation, will judge!"

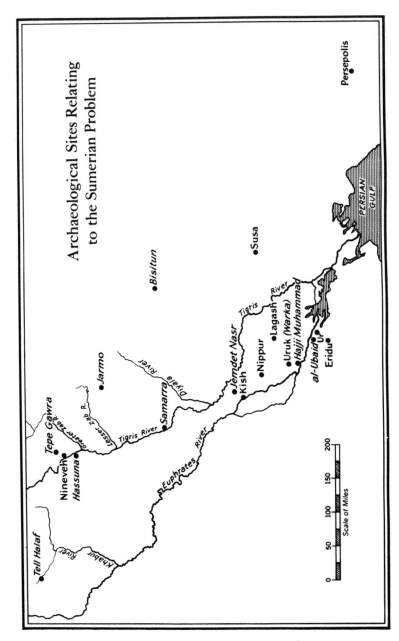

Archaeological Sites Relating
to the Sumerian Problem

Persepolis

PERSIAN GULF

Bisitun

Susa

Tigris River

Lagash
Uruk (Warka)
Hajji Muhammad
al-Ubaid
Ur
Eridu

Jemdet Nasr
Kish

Nippur

Jarmo

Diyala River

Samarra River

Tigris River

Lesser Zab R.

Greater Zab R.

Tepe Gawra

Nineveh
Hassuna

Euphrates River

Tell Halaf

Khabur River

0   50   100   150   200

Scale of Miles

48

PART TWO
The Second Phase: Archaeology

By 1900 philology *alone* could contribute little more to the solution or even the elucidation of the Sumerian Problem. Philologists had discovered the Sumerian language, named it, and established the existence of the Sumerians themselves, but corroborative evidence of a nonphilological sort would be welcome along with any new data from other sources. Fortunately, even before 1900, help was on the way. It came from the finds of the archaeologists, principally from the French at Telloh (Lagash) and the Americans at Nippur.[1] On these two sites, the digging penetrated lower levels than any previously reached and got down to strata of the Sumerian epoch (third millennium B.C.) which lay below the already known Semitic levels of the twenty centuries preceding the Christian era. The cuneiform texts discovered in the lower strata were mostly Sumerian; and this showed—if it needed showing—that Sumerian was a real language once used by real people. The fact that the very earliest documents were entirely Sumerian also seemed to demonstrate the priority of Sumerians over Semites in Mesopotamia.

Nevertheless, it was soon apparent that archaeological data was sometimes more difficult to interpret than the philological evidence. In reaction against the squabbles of the Sumerists and anti-Sumerists, the historian Eduard Meyer, who was neither archaeologist nor philologian, tried a new tack in 1906 in his book entitled *Sumerians and Semites in Babylonia.*[2] The archaeologists had found in the Kassite, Old Babylonian, and Sumerian levels numerous statues, reliefs, plaques, and the like representing the people of Babylonia and their deities. These representations showed a variety of differences in physical appearance and dress,

---

[1] For the excavations, see Kramer, *Sumerians*, pp. 21–32.
[2] E. Meyer, *Sumerier und Semiten in Babylonien*, Berlin, 1906.

and Meyer thought he could distinguish the presence of three types of people in ancient Mesopotamia: (1) the Sumerians, who had shaven heads and smooth-shaven faces; (2) the Semites, who had long hair and beards; and (3) the Bedouin (West Semites) who wore beards but shaved the upper lip and cut their hair short. Meyer observed that the male deities were always portrayed in the Semitic manner with long hair and beards, while the people he had identified as Sumerians shaved their heads and wore no beards. This signified, he reasoned, that the Semites must have occupied Babylonia before the Sumerians arrived, and the latter must have borrowed their deities from the Semites. Religious borrowing was possible and Meyer thought it probable, but the clear-cut cultural superiority of the Sumerians over the early Semites was an obstacle in the path of Meyer's hypothesis. It had been established, for example, that the cuneiform was a Sumerian invention and had been borrowed from the Sumerians by the Semites. If the Sumerians had arrived by way of the Persian Gulf, bringing an already well-developed culture—this was Meyer's theory, was it likely that they would have exchanged their own religion for that of the Semites?

In 1910, the new aspects of the Sumerian Problem were reviewed by L. W. King in his *History of Sumer and Akkad*.[3] King summarized the philological controversy, pointing out that the discovery of unilingual Sumerian texts in the lower strata at Telloh and Nippur had demolished Halévy's arguments. The focus of the Sumerian Problem, said King, had changed:[4]

> That Babylonian civilization and culture originated with the Sumerians is no longer in dispute; the point upon which difference of opinion now centres concerns the period at which Sumerians and Semites first came into contact.

He continued as follows:[5]

[3] L. W. King, *History of Sumer and Akkad*, (London: Chatto and Windus Ltd., 1910).

[4] *Ibid.*, p. 6. (Reprinted by permission of publisher and Author's Literary Estate).

[5] *Ibid.*, pp. 40–43; 47–55.

It is not generally recognized that the two races which inhabited Sumer and Akkad during the early historical periods were sharply divided from one another not only by their speech but also in their physical characteristics. One of the principal traits by which they may be distinguished consists in the treatment of the hair. While the Sumerians invariably shaved the head and face, the Semites retained the hair of the head and wore long beards. A slight modification in the dressing of the hair was introduced by the Western Semites of the First Babylonian Dynasty, who brought with them from Syria the Canaanite Bedouin custom of shaving the lips and allowing the beard to fall only from the chin; while they also appear to have cut the hair short in the manner of the Arabs or Nabateans of the Sinai peninsula. The Semites who were settled in Babylonia during the earlier period, retained the moustache as well as the beard, and wore their hair long. While recognizing the slight change of custom, introduced for a time during the West Semitic domination, the practice of wearing hair and beard was a Semitic characteristic during all periods of history. The phrase "the black-headed ones," which is of frequent occurrence in the later texts, clearly originated as a description of the Semites, in contradistinction to the Sumerians with their shaven heads.

Another distinctive characteristic, almost equally striking, may be seen in the features of the face as represented in the outline engraving and in the sculpture of the earlier periods. It is true that the Sumerian had a prominent nose, which forms, indeed, his most striking feature, but both nose and lips are never full and fleshy as with the Semites. It is sometimes claimed that such primitive representations as occur upon Ur-Ninâ's bas-reliefs, or in Figure 2, are too rude to be regarded as representing accurately an ethnological type. But it will be noted that the same general characteristics are also found in the later and more finished sculptures of Gudea's period. This fact is illustrated by the two black diorite heads of statuettes [shown in Figure 3].

Fig. 2 Figures of early Sumerians, engraved upon fragments of shell, which were probably employed for inlaying boxes, or for ornamenting furniture. Earliest period: from Tello.

In both examples certain archaic conventions are retained, such as the exaggerated line of the eyebrows, and the unfinished ear; but nose and lips are obviously not Semitic, and they accurately reproduce the same racial type which is found upon the earlier reliefs.

A third characteristic consists of the different forms of dress worn by Sumerians and Semites, as represented on the monuments. The earliest Sumerians wore only a thick woollen garment, in the form of a petticoat, fastened round the waist by a band or girdle. The garment is sometimes represented as quite plain, in other cases it has a scolloped fringe or border, while in its most elaborate form it consists of three, four, or five horizontal flounces, each lined vertically and scolloped at the edge to represent thick locks of wool.[6] With the later Sumerian patesis this rough garment has been given up in favour of a great shawl or mantle, decorated with a border, which was worn over the left shoulder, and, falling in straight folds, draped

[6] The women of the earlier period appear to have worn a modified form of this garment, made of the same rough wool, but worn over the left shoulder. On the Stele of the Vultures, Eannatum, like his soldiers, wears the petticoat, but this is supplemented by what is obviously a separate garment of different texture thrown over the left shoulder so as to leave the right arm free; this may have been the skin of an animal worn with the natural hair outside.

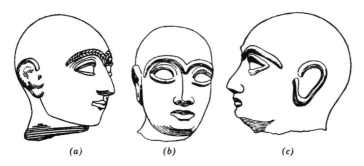

(a)   (b)   (c)

Fig. 3. Later types of Sumerians, as exhibited by heads of male statuettes from Tello. (*b*) and (*c*) are different views of the same head, which probably dates from the age of Gudea; (*a*) may possibly be assigned to a rather later period.

the body with its opening in front.[7] Both these Sumerian forms of garment are of quite different types from the Semitic loin-cloth worn by Narâm-Sin on his stele of victory, and the Semitic plaid in which he is represented on his stele from Pir Hussein. The latter garment is a long, narrow plaid which is wrapped round the body in parallel bands, with the end thrown over the left shoulder. It has no slit, or opening, in front like the later Sumerian mantle, and, on the other hand, was not a shaped garment like the earlier Sumerian flounced petticoat, though both were doubtless made of wool and were probably dyed in bright colours.

Two distinct racial types are thus represented on the monuments, differentiated not only by physical features but also by the method of treating the hair and by dress. Moreover, the one type is characteristic of those rulers whose language was Sumerian, the other represents those whose inscriptions are in the Semitic tongue. Two apparent inconsistencies should here be noted. On the Stele of the Vultures, Eannatum and his soldiers are sculptured with thick hair flowing from beneath their hel-

[7] A very similar fringed mantle was usually worn by the Sumerian women of the later period, but it was draped differently upon the body. Pressed at first over the breasts and under each arm, it is crossed at the back and its ends, thrown over the shoulders, fall in front in two symmetrical points; for a good example of the garment as seen from the front.

mets and falling on their shoulders. But they have shaven faces, and, in view of the fact that on the same monument all the dead upon the field of battle and in the burial mounds have shaven heads, like those of the Sumerians assisting at the burial and the sacrificial rites, we may regard the hair of Eannatum and his warriors as wigs, worn like the wigs of the Egyptians, on special occasions and particularly in battle. The other inconsistency arises from the dress worn by Hammurabi on his monuments. This is not the Semitic plaid, but the Sumerian fringed mantle, and we may conjecture that, as he wrote his votive inscriptions in the Sumerian as well as in the Semitic language, so, too, he may have symbolized his rule in Sumer by the adoption of the Sumerian form of dress.

Professor Meyer has sought to show that the Semites were not only in Babylonia at the date of the earliest Sumerian sculptures that have been recovered, but also that they were in occupation of the country before the Sumerians. The type of the Sumerian gods at the later period is well illustrated by a limestone panel

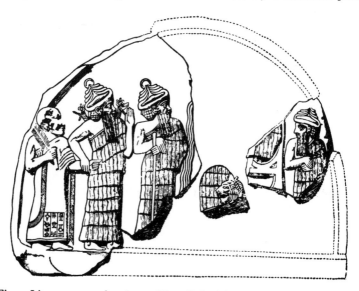

Fig. 4. Limestone panel sculptured in relief, with a scene representing Gudea being led by Ningishzida and another god into the presence of a deity who is seated on a throne.

of Gudea, which is preserved in the Berlin Museum. The sculptured scene is one that is often met with on cylinder-seals of the period, representing a suppliant being led by lesser deities into the presence of a greater god. [see Figure 4]. In this instance Gudea is being led by his patron deity Ningishzida and another god into the presence of a deity who was seated on a throne and held a vase from which two streams of water flow. The right half of the panel is broken, but the figure of the seated god may be in part restored from the similar scene upon Gudea's cylinder-seal [see Figure 5]. There, however, the symbol of the spouting vase is multiplied, for not only does the god hold one in each hand, but three others are below his feet, and into them the water falls and spouts again. Professor Meyer would identify the god of the waters with Anu, though there is more to be said for M. Heuzey's view that he is Enki, the god of the deep. We are not here concerned, however, with the identity of the deities, but with the racial type they represent. It will be seen that they all have hair and beards and wear the Semitic plaid, and from a striking contrast to Gudea with his shaven head and face, and his fringed Sumerian mantle.[8]

Fig. 5. Figure of the seated god on the Cylinder-seal of Gudea.

A very similar contrast is represented by the Sumerian and his gods in the earlier historical periods. Upon the Stele of the Vultures, for instance, the god Ningirsu is represented with abundant hair, and although his lips and cheeks are shaved a long beard falls from below his chin. He is girt around the waist with a plain garment, which is not of the later Semitic type, but the treatment of the hair and beard is obviously not Sumerian. The same bearded type of god is

[8] The fact on seals of this later period the Moon-god is represented in the Sumerian mantle and headdress may well have been a result of the Sumerian reaction, which took place under the kings of Ur.

found upon early votive tablets from Nippur [see Figure 6], and also on a fragment of an archaic Sumerian relief from Tello [see Figure 7], which, from the rudimentary character of the work and the style of the composition, has been regarded as the most ancient example of Sumerian sculpture known. The contours of the figures are vaguely indicated in low relief upon a flat plaque, and the interior details are indicated only by the point. The scene is evidently of a mythological character, for the seated figure may be recognized as a goddess by the horned crown she wears. Beside her stands a god who turns to smite a bound captive with a heavy club or mace. While the captive has the shaven head and face of a Sumerian, the god has abundant hair and a long beard.

Man forms his god in his own image, and it is surprising that the gods of the Sumerians should not be of the Sumerian type. If the Sumerian shaved his own head and face, why should he

Fig. 6. Votive tablets from Nippur, engraved with scenes of worship.

have figured his gods with long beards and abundant hair and
have clothed them with the garments of another race? Professor
Meyer's answer to the question is that the Semites and their
gods were already in occupation of Sumer and Akkad before
the Sumerians came upon the scene. He would regard the Semites
at this early period as settled throughout the whole country, a
primitive and uncultured people with only sufficient knowledge
of art to embody the figures of their gods in rude images of stone
or clay. There is no doubt that the Sumerians were a warrior
folk, and he would picture them as invading the country at a
later date, and overwhelming Semitic opposition by their superior weapons and method of attack. The Sumerian method of
fighting he would compare to that of the Dorians with their
closed phalanx of lance-bearing warriors, though the comparison is not quite complete, since no knowledge of iron is postu-
lated on the part of the Sumerians. He would regard the invaders as settling mainly in the south, driving many of the Semites
northward, and taking over from them the ancient centres of
Semitic cult. They would naturally have brought their own
gods with them, and these they would identify with the deities
they found in possession of the shrines, combining their at-

Fig. 7. Sumerian deities on an archaic relief from Tello.

tributes, but retaining the cult-images, whose sacred character would ensure the permanent retention of their outward form. The Sumerians in turn would have influenced their Semitic subjects and neighbours, who would gradually have acquired from them their higher culture, including a knowledge of writing and the arts.

It may be admitted that the theory is attractive, and it certainly furnishes an explanation of the apparently foreign character of the Sumerian gods. But even from the archaeological side it is not so complete nor so convincing as at first sight it would appear. Since the later Sumerian gods were represented with full moustache and beard, like the earliest figures of Semitic kings which we possess, it would naturally be supposed that they would have this form in the still earlier periods of Sumerian history. But, as we have seen, their lips and cheeks are shaved. Are we then to postulate a still earlier Semitic settlement, of a rather different racial type to that which founded the kingdom of Kish and the empire of Akkad? Again, the garments of the gods in the earliest period have little in common with the Semitic plaid, and are nearer akin to the plainer form of garment worn by contemporary Sumerians. The divine headdress, too, is different to the later form, the single horns which encircle what may be a symbol of the date-palm, giving place to a plain conical headdress decorated with several pairs of horns [see Figure 8].

Thus, important differences are observable in the form of the earlier Sumerian gods and their dress and insignia, which it is difficult to reconcile with Professor Meyer's theory of their origin. Moreover, the principal example which he selected to

(a)   *(b)*   *(c)*

Fig. 8. Earlier and later forms of divine headdresses. (*a*) and (*b*) are from the obverse of the Stele of the Vultures, fragments C and B; (*c*), the later form of horned headdress, is from a sculpture of Gudea.

illustrate his thesis, the god of the central shrine of Nippur, has since been proved never to have borne the Semitic name of Bêl, but to have been known under his Sumerian title of Enlil from the beginning. It is true that Professor Meyer claims that this point does not affect his main argument; but at least it proves that Nippur was always a Sumerian religious centre, and its recognition as the central and most important shrine in the country by Semites and Sumerians alike, tells against any theory requiring a comparatively late date for its foundation.

Such evidence as we possess from the linguistic side is also not in favour of the view which would regard the Semites as in occupation of the whole of Babylonia before the Sumerian immigration. If that had been the case we should naturally expect to find abundant traces of Semitic influence in the earliest Sumerian texts that have been recovered. But, as a matter of fact, no Semitism occurs in any text from Ur-Ninâ's period to that of Lugal-zaggisi with the single exception of a Semitic loan-word on the Cone of Entemena. In spite of the scanty nature of our material, this fact distinctly militates against the assumption that Semites and Sumerians were living side by side in Sumer at the time. But the occurrence of the Semitic word in Entemena's inscription proves that external contact with some Semitic people had already taken place. Moreover, it is possible to press the argument from the purely linguistic side too far. A date-formula of Samsu-iluna's reign has proved that the Semitic speech of Babylonia was known as "Akkadian," and it has therefore been argued that the first appearance of Semitic speech in the country must date from the establishment of Shar-Gani-sharri's empire with its capital at Akkad. But there is little doubt that the Semitic kingdom of Kish, represented by the reigns of Sharru-Gi, Manishtusu and Urumush, was anterior to Sargon's empire, and, long before the rise of Kish, the town of Akkad may well have been the first important centre of Semitic settlement in the north.

It would thus appear that at the earliest period of which remains or records have been recovered, Semites and Sumerians were both settled in Babylonia, the one race in the north, the other southwards nearer the Persian Gulf. Living at first in comparative isolation, trade and war would gradually bring them into closer contact. Whether we may regard the earliest rulers of Kish as Semites like their later successors, is still in doubt. The character of Enbi-Ishtar's name points to his being a Semite; but the still earlier king of Kish, who is referred to on the Stele of the Vultures, is represented on that monument as a Sumerian with shaven head and face. But this may have been due to a convention in the sculpture of the time, and it is quite possible that Mesilim and his successors were Semites, and that their relations with the contemporary rulers of Lagash represent the earlier stages in a racial conflict which dominates the history of the later periods.

Of the original home of the Sumerians, from which they came to the fertile plains of Southern Babylonia, it is impossible to speak with confidence. The fact that they settled at the mouths of the great rivers has led to the suggestion that they arrived by sea, and this has been connected with the story in Berossus of Oannes and the other fish-men, who came up from the Erythraean Sea and brought religion and culture with them. But the legend need not bear this interpretation; it merely points to the Sea-country on the shores of the Gulf as the earliest centre of Sumerian culture in the land. Others have argued that they came from a mountain-home, and have cited in support of their view the institution of the ziggurat or temple-tower, built "like a mountain," and the employment of the same ideogram for "mountain" and for "land." But the massive temple-tower appears to date from the period of Gudea and the earlier kings of Ur, and, with the single exception of Nippur, was probably not a characteristic feature of the earlier temples; and it is now known that the ideogram for "land" and "mountain" was employed in the earlier periods for foreign lands, in contradistinction to that of the Sumerians themselves. But, in spite of the unsoundness of these arguments, it is most probable that the Sumerians did descend on Babylonia from the mountains on the east. Their entrance into the country would thus have been the first of several immigrations from that quarter, due to climatic and physical changes in Central Asia.

Still more obscure is the problem of their racial affinity.

The obliquely set eyes of the figures in the earlier reliefs, due mainly to an ignorance of perspective characteristic of all primitive art, first suggested the theory that the Sumerians were of Mongol type; and the further developments of this view, according to which a Chinese origin is to be sought both for Sumerian roots and for the cuneiform character, are too improbable to need detailed refutation. A more recent suggestion, that their language is of Indo-European origin and structure, is scarcely less improbable, while resemblances which have been pointed out between isolated words in Sumerian and in Armenian, Turkish, and other languages of Western Asia, may well be fortuitous. With the Elamites upon their eastern border the Sumerians had close relations from the first, but the two races do not appear to be related either in language or by physical characteristics. The scientific study of the Sumerian tongue, inaugurated by Professors Zimmern and Jensen, and more especially by the work of M. Thureau-Dangin on the early texts, will doubtless lead in time to more accurate knowledge on this subject; but, until the phonetic elements of the language are firmly established, all theories based upon linguistic comparisons are necessarily insecure.

In view of the absence of Semitic influence in Sumer during the earlier periods, it may be conjectured that the Semitic immigrants did not reach Babylonia from the south, but from the north-west, after traversing the Syrian coast-lands. This first great influx of Semitic nomad tribes left colonists behind them in that region, who afterwards as the Amurru, or Western Semites, pressed on in their turn into Babylonia and established the earliest independent dynasty in Babylon. The original movement continued into Northern Babylonia, and its representatives in history were the early Semitic kings of Kish and Akkad. But the movement did not stop there; it passed on to the foot of the Zagros hills, and left its traces in the independent principalities of Lulubu and Gutiu. Such in outline appears to have been the course of this early migratory movement, which, after colonizing the areas through which it passed, eventually expended itself in the western mountains of Persia. It was mainly through contact with the higher culture of the Sumerians that the tribes which settled in Akkad were enabled later on to play so important a part of the history of Western Asia.

Five years later (1915), the situation seemed little changed. Meyer's thesis was bothersome and seemed to generate the greatest concern. The First World War had interrupted both communications and scholarship and it was not until the twenties that the latest archaeological discoveries (those made between 1900–1914) began to have their effect upon scholarly thought. Thus, the evaluations of Jastrow seemed fair enough when, after the conventional review of the early story, he said:[9]

> Meanwhile, cuneiform texts of the older period were coming to light from mounds in the south, from which it became clear that the Assyrian civilization was merely an offshoot of the culture that arose in the south, in the Euphrates Valley. It was therefore in the south that the solution of the problem as to the origin of the culture and the script was to be sought. Now, as one proceeded backwards, the texts appeared to be more and more ideographic in character. Ere long texts were found which seemed to be entirely ideographic, and such texts increased largely in numbers with the unearthling of the ancient city of Shirpurla (or Lagash) through de Sarzec. The inscriptions on the many statues and votive offerings of Gudea and of other rulers were written in the older style, which scholars now began to regard as Sumerian; and yet even on these monuments Semitic words appeared and again some of the oldest inscriptions of the south were clearly Semitic and not Sumerian.
>
> What did all this mean? If the Sumerians originated the Sumerian culture and were the inventors of the script, we should expect to find the oldest inscriptions to be in Sumerian and, what is more, in pure Sumerian; and it ought also to be possible to reconstruct the original language of the cuneiform script in such a way as to place the language in some definite group, as the Babylonian and the Persian cuneiform had been. Various attempts of this kind to find affiliations between Sumerian and

[9] M. Jastrow, *The Civilization of Babylonia and Assyria*, (Philadelphia: J. B. Lippincott Company, 1915,) pp. 103–107.

Turkish or between Sumerian and some Ural-Altaic groups failed. It was therefore natural that a doubt should have arisen whether the Sumerian represented a real language or whether the Sumerians, if they existed, were the originators of the culture and the inventors of the script. The Sumerian theory manifested at first such weaknesses that one of the most eminent Semitists of his day, Joseph Halévy, was led to put forward the thesis that what scholars regarded as the Sumerian language was nothing but an older ideographic method of writing the Semitic Akkadian or Babylonian, which, in the course of its evolution, had adopted many more or less artificial devices for expressing niceties of thought and grammatical complications. The thesis carried with it the Semitic origin of the Euphratean culture and practically eliminated the Sumerians altogether. Sumer and Akkad as they appeared on the tablets of early rulers in the Euphrates Valley were purely geographical designations of the southern and northern portions of the valley respectively. Even the opponents of Halévy were obliged to admit that he had revealed weak points in the Sumerian theory and it is due to him that Assyriology was deflected from the erroneous direction into which it had turned. It is now admitted that many of the hymns and incantations which scholars had been accustomed to regard as Sumerian are comparatively late compositions, or that they have come down to us in a late revised form betraying Semitic influences. It is also generally admitted to a larger extent than was formerly the case that the Semitic settlers of Babylonia had a large share in perfecting the cuneiform syllabary, that many texts which are written ideographically are in reality Semitic compositions and are to be read as such, and that even in genuine Sumerian texts Semitic influence is apparent; but for all that, evidence sufficient in both quantity and quality has been brought forward to show that the early population of the Euphrates Valley was mixed in character, that by the side of Semites we find a Turanian race clearly depicted on the monuments and demarcated by their physiognomies and by differences of costume from the Semitic population.

We owe to Eduard Meyer the definite establishment of this thesis. On the linguistic side, evidence for the existence of a Sumerian language has recently been brought forward which does not rest upon guesswork or on pure conjecture, but is made conclusive by the study of the oldest texts of Babylonia. As long as Sumerian was simply to be deduced from the ideographic values of the signs, one was justified in doubting whether we were in the presence of a real language, for since ideographs could be read as Semitic as well as Sumerian, it was indeed possible to regard a "Sumerian" inscription as merely another form of writing Babylonian—a very arificial form to be sure and yet, since all writing is a more or less artificial device, a possible form. When, however, the proof was furnished from the texts that Sumerian words could be written phonetically as well as ideographically, that even in Sumerian the device existed of writing a word as in Babylonian either by a single sign representing the word or by signs representing the word or by the signs representing the syllables of which it is composed, there could no longer be any question as to the genuine linguistic character of Sumerian. In addition to the evidence for phonetic writing, which became more and more abundant as scholars penetrated deeper into the study of the oldest texts from ancient Babylonian centres, the proof of a fixed grammatical structure for nouns and verbal forms was furnished in a manner to carry conviction to the minds of those who had hitherto maintained a skeptical or non-committal attitude towards the linguistic evidence.

Taking up now the question who these Sumerians were, an impartial verdict must confess that the problem still remains obscure. We know that they were not Semites; their features as depicted on the monuments reveal a Turanian type, but the term Turanian is too vague to furnish any definite clue. Various indications point to their having come from a mountainous region. They brought the worship of their native gods with them, and the nature of these deities suggests their having had their original seats on the tops of mountains. It is to the Sumerians that we owe the construction of the stage-towers on which remains have been found in all the important centres of Babylonia and Assyria. Built in imitation of mountains with an imitation of a mountain road leading to the sanctuary at the top, it is reasonable to conclude that the thought of housing the gods in this way

arose in the minds of a people accustomed to the worship of
gods whose seats were on mountain peaks. There is other evidence pointing in the same direction of an original mountain
home whence the Sumerians came at a remote period to settle
in the Euphrates Valley. Now there are mountains to the east and
north-east of Babylonia, and it is therefore possible that the
Sumerians entered the Valley from this side—perhaps under
pressure of other mountain hordes coming from the north. But
they may also have come, as has been recently maintained, from
mountainous districts to the northwest of Mesopotamia. Whether
the Sumerians already found the Semites in possession of Babylonia and then conquered them, or whether the Sumerians were
the earliest settlers and founded the culture in that district is
another question that has not been definitely decided, with the
evidence, however, in favor of the view that the Semites were the
first on the ground and that they had already made some advance
in culture when the Sumerians swept down upon them and imposed their rule and such culture as they brought with them on the
older settlers.

Between the two World Wars, the excavation of many old and
new sites brought a rich harvest of new finds. Although the
archaeological wealth thus acquired could definitely be put on
the credit side of the ledger, it was not without its disadvantages. First, the archaeologists were so busy in the field that
it was often years before they published their findings with the
result that important discoveries remained unknown to the scholarly world at large. Second, there was so much material that did
come to light within the space of a few years that it could not
be immediately comprehended in its entirety. The third dis-
advantage was that archaeology had become a specialized discipline—there were even specializations within it, and thus the
outsider, or frequently an archaeologist who had specialized in
one period or one area, was not sufficiently acquainted with the
overall results to be able to generalize about them. On the one
hand, the wealth of new material made it possible to expose
the fallacy of Meyer's thesis: many examples came to light of
known Semites represented as hairless and beardless, and of

known Sumerians with hair and beards. On the other hand, when three giants among the scholars—Wooley, Speiser, and Frankfort —attacked the Sumerian problem, each offered a different solution. This was due partly to the fact that none of them attempted to use all the evidence, yet it was also true that, even if endowed with superhuman competence, as late as 1939 the researcher would have had to conclude that the Sumerian Problem admitted the formulation of several irreconcilable hypotheses.

Sir Leonard Woolley, the great excavator of Ur and Al Ubaid, published in 1928 his popular and widely-read book, *The Sumerians*. With considerable disregard of the work of his predecessors and contemporaries and with a large degree of independence in formulating his own views, Woolley began his book as follows:[10]

> By the second millennium before Christ the formula used by Mesopotamian kings to show that their power extended over the whole Land of the Two Rivers was "King of Sumer and Akkad." The great alluvial plain from the site of the modern city of Baghdad, where the Tigris and the Euphrates approach most closely to each other, down to a point a little below Kurna, where was then the head of the Gulf, was divided into two parts; the boundary between these was ill-defined, shifting this way and that with the vicissitudes of conquest and with the rise and fall of rival elements in the population, but in the main the two countries stood in sharp opposition to one another, distinguished by the race and language of those who lived in them: Akkad, in the north, was predominantly Semitic; Sumer, in the south, was more mixed, but the Semitic element here was swamped by the Sumerians who had imposed on it their language and their civilization and had the land called after their own name.
>
> Lower Mesopotamia, which includes both Sumer and Akkad, is a delta redeemed from the Persian Gulf whose waters once reached nearly as far north as Hit, and it is a delta of very recent formation. The upper Euphrates valley and the high plateau of the Syrian desert had been inhabited by man long before the

[10] C. L. Wooley, *The Summerians*, Oxford: (The Clarendon Press, 1928), pp. 1–13. Reprinted by permission of the publisher.

gùlf waters had receded: there the monuments of the palaeolithic age abound, and the later stone age has left its traces in the
valleys of the Euphrates, the Khabur and the Sajur, but in
Mesopotamia itself nothing of the kind is found: in the earliest
human settlements flint instruments indeed are common, but they
are associated with metal or betray the influence of metal-work-
ing, and we can only conclude that it was comparatively late in
human history, when man had already advanced into the calcho-
lithic age, that the lower valley became fit for his occupation.

Just by the modern town of Muhammerah in Persia, where in
old days stretched the waters of the greater gulf, the river Karun
empties into the Shatt al-Arab. Almost opposite to it is the Wadi
al-Batin, now dry but once a great river running up from the
heart of Arabia. The Karun brings down from the Persian hills
as much silt as do the waters of the Tigris and the Euphrates
combined, and the old al-Batin stream, though more sluggish,
must have been almost as rich in silt; in the course of time the
mud discharged by them into the gulf massed below their
mouths in banks which gradually advancing across the gulf
joined up and made a bar from shore to shore. The bar neutral-
ized the scouring action of the gulf tide and enabled the Tigris
and the Euphrates to deposit at their mouths the silt which had
hitherto been swept out to sea, and at the same time the silt of
the southern rivers began to fill in what had now become a great
lagoon, while the waters of all of them joined in turning it
gradually from salt to brackish and from brackish to fresh. The
mud of the two northern streams that did not go to swell the
delta now forming at their mouths was dropped, now that the
current was checked by the bar, over the whole of the old gulf
area and helped to raise the level of its bed; thus, while dry
land was formed first and most quickly in the north and in the
south, the lagoon between grew more and more shallow, islands
appeared, and at last where all had been a waste of water there
stretched a vast delta of clay and sand and mud, diversified by
marshes and reed-beds, through which wound rivers so flush with
their banks that they were forever changing their courses: it was
a delta periodically flooded, and in the summer scorched by a

pitiless sun, but its soil, light and stoneless, was as rich as could be found anywhere on earth, and scarcely needed man's labour to produce man's food. The description in Genesis of the creation of the earth as man's home agrees admirably with the process of the formation of the Mesopotamian delta: "Let the waters under the heaven be gathered together unto one place, and let the dry land appear: and it was so. . . . And the earth brought forth grass, and herb yielding seed after his kind, and the tree yielding fruit, whose seed was in itself, after his kind: and God saw that it was good."

The manner in which the land formed is important as serving to explain the differences in the population that occupied it. A country so rich potentially invited settlers, and these were forthcoming, but they must have come in gradually as the process of transformation took place, and they did not come from the same regions, but from all the shores of the ancient gulf.

The northern part of the Syrian desert and the upper Euphrates valley were inhabited by a people of Semitic speech known, when they first appear in history, as the Martu or, later, as the Amurru. It was natural that as the delta formed in the north at the mouth of the Euphrates the new land should be colonized by these neighbouring folk following the retreating waters and cultivating the freshly-dried alluvium: they occupied Sippar and Opis, on either side of the neck of land where the two rivers come closest together, and thereby secured possession of the northern triangle which was to be the land of Akkad. To the north and east of them, in the Zagros hills and across the plain to the Tigris, there lived a people of a very different stock, fair-haired and speaking a "Caucasian" tongue, a hill-people akin to the Guti who were to play no small part in Sumerian history; they seem to have moved down into the Tigris valley, but their advance south was blocked by the Martu occupation of the land neck, so that they failed to gain a footing in the new delta and remained in what was afterwards Assyria, the neighbour land to Akkad.

Scattered over the central Arabian plateau were the ancestors of the modern Beduin and these nomads also took advantage of the rich opportunities offered by the drying up of the lower delta to change their mode of life, individual families or clans drifting down from the desert uplands into the marshes wherever an island site made agriculture possible. Thus into Sumer there came a Semitic element which was quite distinct from the Semitic population of Akkad; except for a similarity of language (and even here the dialects must have been very different) they had little in common with them and certainly had not attained anything like the same degree of civilization. The colonists of Akkad, coming from a comparatively civilized home-land with which they needed not to lose touch, were better organized and capable of common action, so that city life would have been possible from the beginning: the southern Semites were strangers to town life, owing to the nature of the marshy country their occupation of it would tend to be more sporadic, and both character and circumstances would prevent such social unity as would enable them to hold their own against neighbours better equipped.

The last of the incomers were the Sumerians. These were a dark-haired people—"black-heads," the texts call them—speaking an agglutinative language somewhat resembling ancient Turkish (Turanian) in its formation though not in its etymology; judging by their physical type they were of the Indo-European stock, in appearance not unlike the modern Arab,[11] and were certainly

[11] The Mesopotamian peoples, both past and present, represent a transition between Iranian and Semitic types, but they have retained more of the Iranian than of the Semite. . . . As to the racial nature of the al-'Ubaìd people there cannot be any doubt; if they were living to-day we should call them Arabs. . . . There is no trace . . . of any round-headed element of the Hittite type nor of a Mongolian type. . . . The southern Mesopotamians at the beginning of the fourth millennium B.C. had big, long and narrow heads; their affinities were with the peoples of the Caucasian or European type, and we may regard south-western Asia as their cradleland until evidence leading to a different conclusion comes to light. They were akin to the predynastic people of Egypt described by Dr. Foquet, but differed from all other predynastic and dynastic Egyptians. The Neolithic people of English long barrows were also related to them—perhaps distantly; the Sumerian type made its appearance in Europe in Palaeolithic times, for one of the earliest of Aurignacian skulls—that found at Combe Capelle in the Dordogne, France, is near akin to the ancient Arab type." Sir Arthur Keith in *Al-'Ubaid*, pp. 216, 240.

well developed intellectually. What their original home was we do not know. The fact that Sumerian gods are constantly represented as standing upon mountains would imply that the people came from a hill country; that their earliest building style is based on a tradition of timber construction is an argument to the same conclusion, for such could only originate in the heavily-timbered uplands; the description given in Genesis, "and the people journeyed from the east and came into the plain of Shinar and dwelt there," refers to the Sumerians and must incorporate some Sumerian legend as to their own movements; but the obvious conclusion that they descended from the Elamite mountains which border the delta valley on the east does not meet the case, for though there are common elements in the early cultures of Mesopotamia and Elam it does not seem possible to derive the Sumerian from the latter, nor does the physical type show identity of race: Sumerian legends which explain the beginnings of civilization in Mesopotamia seem to imply an influx of people from the sea, which people can scarcely be other than the Sumerians themselves, and the fact that the historic Sumerians are at home in the south country and that Eridu, the city reputed by them to be the oldest in the land, is the southernmost of all, supports that implication. Sir Arthur Keith states:[12] "One can still trace the ancient Sumerian face eastwards among the inhabitants of Afghanistan and Baluchistan, until the valley of the Indus is reached—some 1,500 miles distant from Mesopotamia." Recent excavation in the Indus valley has brought to light extensive remains of a very early civilization remarkably developed, which has a good deal in common with that of Sumer; particularly striking are rectangular stamp seals found in the two countries which are identical in form, in the subjects and style of their engraving, and in the inscriptions which they bear, while there are similarities hardly less marked in terra-cotta figures, in the methods of building construction and in ground-plans. To say that these resemblances prove identity of race or even political unity would be to exaggerate the weight of the evidence; to account for them by mere trade connexion would be, in my

[12] *Al-'Ubaid*, p. 216.

opinion, to underrate it no less rashly: it is safest, for the time being, to regard the two civilizations as offshoots from a common source which presumably lies somewhere between the Indus and the Euphrates valleys, though whether the centre from which this culture radiates so far afield is to be sought in the hills of Baluchistan, or where, we have no means of knowing as yet.

There is another factor which further complicates the question. The oldest levels yet tapped in southern Mesopotamia produce a very fine painted pottery which disappears entirely before the beginning of the historic period as we know it, i.e. before the earliest of the graves at Ur which must date to about 3500 B.C. The pots are hand-made or, more rarely, turned on the slow-moving wheel, the *tournette*; the walls, of greenish grey, buff or red ware, are sometimes extremely thin, and are ornamented with a decoration built up from simple geometric motives executed in a brown or black semi-lustrous paint. Between this pottery and that found in the lowest levels at Susa, at Musyan in Elam and at Bushire on the Persian Gulf, there are points of resemblance which undoubtedly connote a certain relation and have by some writers been taken to prove a close parentage; actually there are also points of difference which make such close parentage impossible. The Mesopotamian ware is older in time than the Elamite and belongs to a considerably earlier stage of development, so that it cannot be derived from the Elamite; consequently it supplies no evidence for the Sumerians being descended from Elam. Further, we cannot even be sure that the Mesopotamian pottery is Sumerian at all: Campbell Thompson, who first drew attention to it at Eridu, considered it to be pre-Sumerian, and this may very well be true. At a place called Jemdet Nasr near Kish painted pottery distinct from that of the southern Sumerian sites, later in date and more nearly resembling the Musyan wares, has been found associated with very early clay tablets inscribed with a semi-pictographic script, but this discovery only proves that at Kish painted pottery survived into the period of Sumerian culture, it does not establish its authorship. As painted wares of very early date also having points of resemblance to and of difference from those of southern Mesopotamia occur further to the north and as far west as

Carchemish, where a Sumerian population cannot have existed at that time, the case for the Sumerian origin of the Mesopotamian pottery is weakened and that for the Elamite origin of the Sumerian people disappears. Who then can have been responsible for this distinctive and almost sole surviving product of the earliest occupation of the lower river valley? It is highly improbable that the finely made and beautifully decorated pottery of Eridu, Ur and al-'Ubaid was the handiwork of Semitic colonists from central Arabia; desert nomads are by reason of their manner of life unready potters, and what we know of later Arabian pottery would not lead us to suspect so artistic a beginning. Perhaps the real clue is given by the parallels noted in the far north. At Ur we have found a crude painted clay figurine of a man, contemporary with the decorated vases, who wears a long thin pointed beard quite unlike anything represented on the oldest Sumerian works of art but curiously like certain figures on mother-of-pearl inlays from Kish, which is an Akkadian, not a Sumerian centre; the painted pottery may be of Akkadian origin. In that case its occurrence at Eridu and Ur may mean that the Martu, who, for all that their speech in historic times was Semitic, must have been of Asia Minor stock, pushed down further south than has been supposed and controlled the country and its scattered population of Arabian colonists as far as the shores of the Persian Gulf, that, in other words, an Akkadian Mesopotamia preceded the incoming of the Sumerians and that the division of the land as we know it later resulted from the driving back of its earliest rulers by invaders from the sea.

Of the three elements then the Sumerians were probably the last to enter the south country. They came from a distance and were not likely to be tempted to migrate so far until the land was sufficiently formed to offer reasonable facilities for agriculture and for commernce, whereas the Semitic nomads were on the spot and would naturally have moved down on to the fertile soil as it appeared. "Mankind when created did not know of bread for eating or garments for wearing. The people walked with limbs on the ground, they are herbs with their mouths like sheep, they drank ditch-water," says a Sumerian hymn, and the description, which scarcely fits the Sumerians themselves as the apostles of civilization, would be apt enough for the despised dwellers in the swamps whom the new-comers found on their arrival and enslaved to their service.

A far cry from Woolley's *Sumerians*, two much more sophisticated and also widely differing interpretations were offered by Ephraim Speiser (1930)[13] and Henri Frankfort (1932).[14] Speiser combined the results of more recent philological research with what he knew of the latest archaeological evidence in an effort to establish that neither the Sumerians nor the Semites had been the earliest inhabitants of Mesopotamia. The central thesis of his monograph, said Speiser, was that "nearly all of the hitherto unclassified cultures and peoples of the ancient Near East can be organized into a single, genetically interrelated, group; the members of that group formed the basic population of Hither Asia, produced the earliest civilizations, and have continued to this day to furnish its ethnic background."[15] Speiser included in his "single genetically interrelated group" all the speakers of "Caucasian" or "Japhethite" languages: principally Elamite, Hurrian, Vannic, and Kurdish. Earlier scholars had noticed that Sumerian etymologies could not be found for the names of the oldest towns in the lower Mesopotamian valley; these were the towns mentioned in the "king lists" as having been the seats of royal power "before the flood." If some people other than the Sumerians had named these towns, then it seemed likely that these "other people" had inhabited the land before the Sumerians arrived. Speiser argued that the names of at least four out of six of the oldest towns—Larak, Shuruppak, Zimbir, and Zarar—appeared to be of Elamite origin. Combining linguistic material of this kind with what was then known of the archaeological evidence, Speiser concluded that the earliest inhabitants of the lower Mesopotamian plain were "Proto-Elamites." The Sumerians, he said, arrived in Sumer (southern Babylonia at the head of the Persian Gulf) only a few hundred years before the beginning of the historic period (about 3000 B.C.); at

[13] E. A. Speiser, *Mesopotamian Origins*, Philadelphia, 1930.
[14] H. Frankfort, "Archeology and the Sumerian Problem," *Studies in Ancient Oriental Civilization*, No. 4, Chicago, 1932.
[15] Speiser, *op. cit.*, p. vii.

the same time an unidentified group invaded Akkad (northern Babylonia). Speiser himself had no theory about the homeland of the Sumerians, merely noting that other scholars had suggested Arabia, India, and Transcaspia.

Unlike Speiser, Frankfort's approach was almost exclusively archaeological, and it was based on a better and more current knowledge of the excavations then in progress. We shall discuss the results of these excavations presently; for the moment it will be sufficient to note that by 1931 it was believed that the prehistory of the lower Tigris-Euphrates valley could be divided into three cultural phases named Ubaid, Uruk, and Jemdet Nasr after the archaeological site where each had been originally discovered. The earliest in the sequence was the Ubaid, found by Woolley; next came Uruk (Warka); and last, Jemdet Nasr, which just preceded the beginning of the historic (Early Dynastic) period. Speiser, incidentally, had been acquainted only with the Ubaid and Jemdet Nasr cultures: he concluded, as we have seen, that the Sumerians had arrived in the Jemdet Nasr period. Frankfort agreed that the Sumerians were present in the Jemdet Nasr period, but he insisted that they were also present in the lower valley in the Uruk phase and had actually inaugurated the habitation of the region in the Ubaid period. Frankfort based his argument on what he interpreted as a continuity of culture in the south. The Sumerians, he said, were known to be in Sumer in the Early Dynastic Age. Since there was no cultural break between the Early Dynastic and the Jemdet Nasr, the Sumerians must have been there in Jemdet Nasr times. Vague and incomplete skeletal evidence seemed to connect the Sumerians with Iran, and the pottery of the Ubaid period had Iranian connections. The Sumerians, argued Frankfort, must have arrived in the Ubaid period. They could not have been the bearers of the intrusive and intervening Uruk culture, the characteristic pottery of which had northern and Anatolian affiliations. This Uruk pottery was associated with areas where Japhethite languages were spoken, and, since Sumerian was not of the Japhethite group, the Sumerians could not have arrived during the Uruk phase.

It was mostly in the years *after* Frankfort published his monograph that the results of certain major excavations concerned with prehistoric Mesopotamian remains began to be published and thus made available to everyone. Al Ubaid (1927) and Jemdet Nasr (1931) were known before 1932, but the publication of the material from other sites came later: Uruk (1932), Nineveh (1933), Tell Halaf (1933), Tepe Gawra (1935), and Hassuna (1945). Actually, the great mass of evidence on prehistory was not fully organized into coherent form until Ann Perkins in 1949 published her invaluable *Comparative Archaeology of Early Mesopotamia.*[16] However, by 1939, it was possible to see that the views of Speiser and Frankfort with regard to the archaeological material had to be revised, and a general outline of Mesopotamian prehistory could be discerned even though the details were uncertain.

In 1939, the accepted view was that there were five main cultural periods beginning with a Neolithic peasant-village stage and running down to the opening of the historic period (Early Dynastic). The two earliest phases, Neolithic (later called Hassuna) and Halaf were in evidence only in the north, in Assyria. The Ubaid culture was the first known in the south, while in the north it followed the Halaf phase. It was only in the Ubaid period that Assyria and Babylonia seemed to share a common culture: the earlier phases, Hassuna and Halaf, were confined to Assyria, and the last two phases in the south (Uruk and Jemdet Nasr) were not known in the north where a separate course was followed after the Ubaid period.

Distinctive kinds of pottery characterized the strata of the various periods and with the pottery were associated certain culture traits or definite cultural assemblages. With pottery of the Neolithic, or Hassuna, type, one found settled peasant villages with domesticated plants and animals, houses of rammed mud, spindle whorls (indicating textile manufacture), and large pots used for grain storage. In the Halaf levels, a new kind of pottery, clay figurines, copper beads, and stamp seals—to mention only a few culture traits—were characteristic. Ubaid pottery was again different; along with it were found the begin-

---

[16] A. L. Perkins, "The Comparative Archeology of Early Mesopotamia," *Studies in Ancient Oriental Civilization*, No. 25, Chicago, 1949.

nings of temple architecture, "bent nails" of clay, sickles of terra cotta, and so on. Uruk pottery was not decorated with painted designs but was a red or gray monochrome ware; the associated culture traits were wheeled vehicles, stone vessels, the use of gold as well as copper, cylinder seals, the development of temple compounds, and a rudimentary "ziggurat." Painted pottery came back in the Jemdet Nasr phase, but far more important were the appearance of writing and the growth of towns into near cities.

Reflecting on the new discoveries, Speiser modified his views. His 1939 article, reprinted below, is admittedly technical; its inclusion here is deliberate with the purpose of demonstrating that the Sumerian Problem has never been child's play. The most important part of the argument is found in Part III where, in language understandable even to the layman, he shows the difficulty of Frankfort's hypothesis.[17]

THE BEGINNINGS OF CIVILIZATION IN MESOPOTAMIA
E. A. SPEISER
UNIVERSITY OF PENNSYLVANIA

In attempting an analysis of so composite a problem as the beginnings of civilization in Mesopotamia, I shall treat the subject under three heads: material elements; social elements; the underlying ethnic forces.

I. MATERIAL ELEMENTS

Our knowledge of predynastic, or proto-historic, Mesopotamia is almost entirely a contribution of the present decade. At the Eighteenth International Congress of Orientalists, held in Leiden in 1931, three archaic stages were established for Lower Mesopotamia. They are, working back from recorded dynastic times,

[17] E. A. Speiser, "The Beginnings of Civilization in Mesopotamia," *Journal of the American Oriental Society*, **LIX** (1939), supplement IV, pp. 17–31. Reprinted by permission of the American Oriental Society.

1. The Jemdet Nasr period
2. The Uruk period
3. The Obeid period

These divisions, as they are generally understood, are at once cultural and chronological. They follow in a definite order, without intervening gaps, and each contains certain characteristic material elements which were first observed on the site that has given its name to the culture in question. The beginning of the Early Dynastic period may now be dated to about 3000 B.C.,[18] with a much smaller margin of error than the round date might imply. Since the three predynastic stages are represented by a total of nearly twenty building levels,[19] the time assigned to the age as a whole could scarcely be less than the entire fourth millennium. The chronology is relative, of course, since much of the age under discussion belongs to the preliterate era. But this relative chronology is abundantly established, and is being constantly confirmed, by the collective testimony of a number of widely distributed ancient centers; so much so that the terms "Jemdet Nasr," "Uruk," and "Obeid" have been adopted for Upper Mesopotamia as well, and they are employed in a restricted sense for other sections of Western Asia, notably Persia, Syria, and Palestine.

Upper Mesopotamia was inhabited long before the alluvial valley of the south had become suitable for human occupation. Whereas the oldest established civilization of Lower Mesopotamia was the one known as "Obeid," separated by two other cultures from the Early Dynastic stage, ancient Assyria has yielded at least two additional stages:

4. The Halaf-Samarra period
5. The Sakjegözü, or Neolithic period

---

[18] See H. Frankfort, *Orient. Inst. Comm.* 20 (1936), Comment on the Chronological Table (after pl. viii). A useful survey of the protohistoric material will be found in Viktor Christian's *Altertumskunde des Zweistromlandes* I, fasc. 2 (1938), although Christian's dates are at times highly individual. See also Th. J. Meek, in *The Haverford Symposium on Archaeology and the Bible* (1938), 158 ff.

[19] E.g., Uruk, archaic II-XVIII.

The last-named stage takes us back, even on conservative estimates, well into the fifth millennium.

For our present purposes, the internal characteristics of each of
the above five predynastic periods are immaterial. Their distin-
guishing features may be ascertained from several general
summaries[20] or, better still, from the original reports on the
various excavations in question. Nor need we dwell on the
principal accomplishments of the predynastic age as a whole,
beyond indicating that the beginnings of building and pottery
lie still farther behind,[21] but that the introduction of metal, the
wheel, the cylinder seal, and writing fall within the predynastic
age of Mesopotamia. It will be of more immediate concern to us
to concentrate instead on correlations of a methodological and
general anthropological nature. These correlations will be stated
briefly in the succeeding paragraphs.

a. First there is a question as to the nature of the divisions into
which predynastic Mesopotamia has been broken up. The terms
currently in use to designate those divisions were first applied to
strictly localized remains which enjoyed prominence over a limited
period of time. Thus "Obeid" was applied originally to a highly
specialized type of painted pottery which was confined to a section of Lower Mesopotamia and flourished until the appearance
in the same region of pottery without painted designs. Secondarily,
the term was applied also to the material context with which
Obeid pottery occurred. In this manner one designation served
for a characteristic product, a period, and a cultural context. It
was adequate so long as the early civilization which it was meant
to signify appeared to remain in comparative isolation. But the
one conclusion towards which all recent archaeological discoveries and researches in Western Asia converge is that even the

[20] See note 18.
[21] That is to say, they are earlier than the deepest stratified deposits
known from Mesopotamia. The stage in question has been reported from
J. Garstang's excavations at Jericho, and may be anticipated from his discoveries at Mersin.

In grouping together the Halaf and Samarra deposits I have had in mind
only their relative chronology. On contextual grounds Samarra proves to
be an early phase of the Obeid-Susa I group.

oldest civilizations of that area were not narrowly localized. Obeid pottery and terracottas are now known also from Upper Mesopotamia, while Obeid decorative motives have correspondences with designs on pottery of the Amri stage, in the Indus Valley, too intricate to be explained away by mere coincidence. If we extend the term "Obeid" to cover Upper Mesopotamia, we shall find it awkward and misleading when applied to a substantial residue of northern remains, including pottery, which have no counterpart in the south. In such circumstances the label in question could be justified only for chronological purposes. "Obeid" would designate a period characterized by a sum of material remains varying in origin and relationship. For a single group of material remains is often insufficient to establish synchronism. The suggested decorative correspondences between Obeid and Amri may point indeed to a common source, but reflect widely separated periods, because the Amri stage is much later than Obeid proper. Careful distinction must be made, therefore, between cultural synchronism and parallels from different periods. The Obeidoid material from the Indus Valley[22] seems to indicate a late survival from a common source.

b. We come back now to the material contents of the five predynastic stages of Mesopotamia. It has been indicated that in Upper Mesopotamia products from the Obeid province in the south mingled with others which were restricted to the north. For instance, the graceful beakers from Gawra 13 do not occur in Obeid proper. They have, however, their analogues in the tumblers from Susa I. On the other hand, Gawra and Obeid share a number of designs which do not occur in Susa. Correlation of the remains from the above three areas, Upper and Lower Mesopotamia and Elam, indicates an underlying relationship among the three which is less apparent when only two of these regions are compared. We now see that the treatment of the human figure was the same in all three provinces. The terracotta figurines from contemporary Ur have the same animal

[22] I would compare, for example, the motives published by N. G. Majumdar in *Mem. of the Arch. Survey of India* 48 (1934), pl. xxxviii, 1-8 (called to my attention by Dr. Marian Welker) with Gawra XIII; see provisionally BASOR 66. 11.

heads as the incised figures on the seals from Gawra and the
painted figures on the pottery from Susa.[23] The obvious mastery
of the artist over his medium, whether it was clay, stone, or
paint, shows clearly that the distortion of the head was inten-
tional. The human representations in question had in each instance
a magic significance. The correspondence between the respective
cultures embraces thus art and religion as well as industry.
There is here a deeper unity that outweighs existing material
differences. But these differences cannot be ignored.[24] At Gawra,
for example, the designs on the pottery of the Obeid period
point in many directions. There are here survivals from earlier
stages (Halaf-Sammarra); elements paralleled in the south, and
others which betray yet another source.[25] The picture of a larger
civilization covering a wide area is thus modified constantly
by sectional peculiarities arising from differences of physical
background and from local traditions and contacts. It is an ever
changing picture of expanse, interaction, and modification. In
each period there is a similarity of outline, but the component
elements may be heterogeneous.

c. With the realization that each age was culturally composite
we begin to appreciate the danger of making this or that mani-
festation of the period characteristic of the entire stage. It is
known, for instance, that the introduction of the cylinder seal
and the consequent emergence of writing took place towards
the end of Uruk times.[26] Does this mean that the inventors of the
cylinder seal were necessarily the authors of the Uruk civiliza-

---

[23] For the figurines from Ur see L. Legrain, *Gazette des Beaux-Arts*
Oct. 1932, p. 142; for Gawra there are stamp seals from Levels XI (post-
Obeid) and XIII which show an analogous treatment of the human figure
with similar distortion of the head; for Susa, cf. E. Pottier, *Mém. de la
Déllég. en Perse* 13 (1912), fig. 129.

[24] For the differences between north and south which were apparent before the discovery of Gawra XIII see M. E. L. Mallowan's summary in
Excavations at Tall Arpachiyah (1935), 70.

[25] BASOR 66. 12.

[26] Falkenstein, *Archaische Texte aus Uruk* (1936), 3. Although Uruk
IVb may be assigned on internal grounds to the Jemdet Nasr period, the
required stage of transition from cylinder seal to tablet makes it necessary
to put the process back to the end of Uruk times.

tion? By no means. The Uruk stage has disclosed internal differences of sufficient magnitude to call for a subdivision into
Uruk A and Uruk B.[27] It is therefore inherently improbable
that the people of Uruk A were alone responsible for the innovations that mark Uruk B. These innovations argue, rather, the
arrival of a new ethnic element. It should be noted in passing,
however, that the ethnic factor is not automatically instru-
mental in bringing about a complete change in an established
civilization. For Uruk A is not eliminated with the appearance of
Uruk B. Similar co-existence of disparate cultural features, which
point conclusively to more than one source, is especially notice-
able in the Jemdet Nasr period.

  d. We see then that the predynastic periods represent units
only in a wide sense. Nor is the line of demarcation between
two given periods clear and sharp. There is an appreciable overlap of Halaf and Obeid, Obeid and Uruk, and Uruk and Jemdet
Nasr. This overlap imparts a flexible character even to chronological boundaries. The fact is thus emphasized that from the
very beginning cultural continuity had a significant part in the shap-
ing of Mesopotamian civilizations. New periods may have been
due to combinations of economic and ethnic forces, but vital
achievements of a preceding stage were also assimilated and
continued. In the light of these facts early civilizations may be
defined as totals of integrated cultural elements which reach
their peak in time and converge in space towards a central core.
There are no sharp chronological or geographical boundaries.
This definition enables us to contrast adequately such successive
stages as Obeid and Uruk, as well as contemporary civilizations
like those of Mesopotamia and Egypt of, say, Jemdet Nasr
times. When contemporary civilizations are thus contrasted, the
surprising result is not that there are palpable differences
between them, but rather that the respective levels of the civilizations compared are essentially similar, provided that intercom-
munication between them existed. Predynastic Egypt and
Mesopotamia differ materially as to contents. But the tempo of
progress shows no corresponding disparity. Qualitative similari-

[27] *4. Vorl. Bericht, Uruk* (1932), 44.

ties alone, as opposed to contextual relationship, cannot always be explained by the all too easy recourse to invasions. Their cause must be sought in a force of a different nature. That force is diffusion.

  e. It is surely no mere coincidence that predynastic times come to an end both in Egypt and Mesopotamia at about the same period; that metal is worked in both countries in very early settlements and that metallurgical advance shows a similar rate of progress in the valleys of the Two Rivers and the Nile; or that cylinder seals link distant areas in Jemdet Nasr times.[28] Diffusion presupposes, of course, physical contact, but the mechanism of diffusion functions freely in times of peace. The need of raw materials, such as obsidian and copper, stimulated commerce, and the barter of goods had as its inevitable corollary the interchange of ideas. Since there were commercial links between early Egypt and Mesopotamia, news of progress in non-negotiable items was also communicated from one region to the other.[29] In view of this it is naive to assume, as has actually

[28] See H. Frankfort, *Cylinder Seals* (1939), 224 ff.

[29] The origin of Egyptian writing can scarcely be viewed in any other light. Its ultimate, though indirect, dependence on Mesopotamian writing is indicated by the following considerations. There are hundreds of Mesopotamian tablets from predynastic times as against the single possible instance of the Lion Hunt palette in Egypt with its two written symbols (On this subject see H. Ranke, *Sber. Heid. Ak. Wiss.* 1924–25, 3 Abh.). According to Siegfried Schott (in Kurt Sethe's *Vom Bilde zum Buchstaben* [1939] 82) there is nothing in the Egyptian system of writing that points to a long period of development, whereas the evolution of Mesopotamian writing is abundantly illustrated from its very beginning. Moreover, the cylinder seal (admittedly of Mesopotamian origin) provides the link between picture and script; and Mesopotamian economy (which differs markedly from Egyptian economy in historic times) furnishes an all but automatic explanation for transforming elements of design into elements of script (Falkenstein, op. cit. 32–3, 47). Finally, there is ample evidence of contacts between Mesopotamia and Egypt at the time of the evolution of Mesopotamian writing (A. Scharff, *Zeit. f. äg. Spr.* 71.89 ff.). But all this indicates no more than that the idea of writing was borrowed by Egypt (for this possibility see Schott, op. cit. 81). In form, the two scripts are strictly independent. Both are based on native artistic elements and the derivative scripts are as different as the respective art styles of Mesopotamia and Egypt.

been done, that plain pottery was invented in Jericho, or that painted wares originated at Tell Halaf. In most cases, the source of a significant invention is lost to us entirely. At best, we may be able to trace a specialized invention to a given area, but hardly to a single site. We have reason to say that the potter's wheel is of Asiatic origin and that the cylinder seal is Mesopotamian. But we cannot prove that the cylinder seal was invented in Uruk, merely by pointing to the fact that the earliest known cylinders have been dug up at Uruk. Such items spread much too quickly to betray us, thousands of years later, not only the civilization that produced them but also the very spot where they originated.

The spread of the knowledge of metals is a case in point. The collective testimony of a number of sites shows that copper was rare in the early phases of the Obeid period, increasing gradually in use until the technique of metallurgy is mastered by Jemdet Nasr times. The art of working copper could not have been discovered on the sites where the metal is first encountered for the simple reason that those sites are not close to copper deposits. It must have been introduced from the outside. Once discovered, however, that art spread rapidly throughout the civilized world, to all areas which maintained contact with one another. The same is true of many subsequent stages of metallurgical progress. The underlying principle of diffusion enables us now to utilize those technological stages as so many chronological criteria. It follows that Susa I or Ghassûl, with their relatively high copper technique, cannot be as old as the Halaf period, in which knowledge of metals can scarcely be said to exist at all.[30]

It goes without saying that the still useful terms "Neolithic" and "Chalcolithic" presuppose, at least to a certain extent, the chronological application of the principle of diffusion. But we should bear in mind that incidental factors attendant upon diffusion must not be ignored. Not all goods popular with one civilization were welcomed necessarily by a neighboring culture. Moreover, synchronisms furnished through diffusion have to be corrected in accordance with the lag involved in each instance,[31]

[30] Cf. JAOS 58 (1938). 672-3.
[31] A considerable time lag is involved, for example, in the spread of the "chalice ware" from Central Persia to the Nineveh area. On the other

and that requires clear evidence as to the respective centers of the elements diffused. In questions of this sort in particular much work remains to be done.

f. So far we have been preoccupied in the main with the dynamics of proto-historic civilizations. With the above remarks in mind, we may now sum up briefly the external characteristics of the predynastic periods of Mesopotamia. The beginning is represented in Gawra 26 and Nineveh 1 by a Neolithic occupation which is paralleled in Judeideh 14, in Northern Syria. It is not the absolute beginning of settled life, because the introduction of building and pottery had already been left behind. The first settlements of Mesopotamia were due, therefore, to outsiders.[32] The succeeding Halaf period is given over to an advanced civilization with technically developed polychrome fabrics, terracotta figurines, amulets, and the first stamp seals.[33] Halaf has its center of concentration in Northern Syria and its settlements do not extend beyond the Tigris. Along that boundary it is met by an eastern culture, whose early manifestations known as Samarra coincide with the end of the Halaf period. Compromises between the two cultures are demonstrable along the line of contact, but the river barrier is not crossed far in either direction, except by scattered importations. Later phases of the eastern culture occupy the Obeid-Susa period. Metal work is introduced and in the north temple architecture flourishes. The synthesized heritage of the Samarra-Obeid-Susa age is assimilated and gradually transformed in the succeeding Uruk stage, under repeated outside influences which result at length in the cultural separation of the north from the south.[34] Henceforward the two

hand, the diffusion of the cylinder from Lower Mesopotamia required comparatively little time to reach Elam and Syria.

[32] On the possible western origin of these outsiders further information may be expected from Garstang's excavations at Mersin.

[33] Gawra has yielded a charred impression of a stamp seal with an excellent design of an ibex, clearly datable to Halaf times. On the problematical date of the cylinder from Chagar Bazar (*Iraq* 3, pl. i 5) see Frankfort, *Cylinder Seals* 228.

[34] Gawra XI-VIII must be treated as a separate culture province in spite of the links with Uruk VI-IV, which testify to the chronological relation-

provinces pursue divergent courses, although lively intercourse
tends to level existing differences. The end of the Uruk period
witnesses in the south the introduction of the cylinder seal and
script. The period comes to an end with the arrival of a new
type of painted pottery, probably from the west,[35] and this
pottery typifies externally the following Jemdet Nasr stage.
Industry and commerce contribute to the growing wealth of
Sumer, which trades now with the rest of Western Asia and
with Egypt. Links with Elam are especially close, and the
influence of the south is now felt in Upper Mesopotamia. Out
of this syncretistic culture there emerges presently the historic
civilization of Sumer, which is to leave a permanent mark not
only on the rest of Mesopotamia and Western Asia but indirectly
also on the classical world and the world of today.

II. SOCIAL ELEMENTS

The earliest civilizations of Mesopotamia have to be judged
entirely by their material remains. Light on social developments
is scanty and incidental. It is reflected by such products as religious architecture, votive objects, and burial customs. Definite
information on social conditions and social organization can
be furnished only by epigraphic sources, and the earliest records
known until recently represent the dynastic levels of Mesopotamia. Today we are able to extend our investigation to predynastic times and reach through the Jemdet Nasr stage to the
last phase of the Uruk period. The results are illuminating indeed.

It has been known for a long time that the Sumerians had left
an indelible impression on succeeding civilizations. Their influ-

---

ship of the two areas. Von Soden has proposed the term "Gawra culture"
for the northern province (Der alte Orient 37 ½, p. 9), but his archaeological interpretation of the culture in question is wholly inadequate.

[35] I am referring here only to the polychrome geometric decoration of the
period. For the naturalistic elements, as represented in the later Diyala
ware, the source must be sought in the Susa II" group, to use Frankfort's
definition of it (Archaeology and the Sumerian Problem [1932] 69).

ence came to be felt in language and literature, law and government, religion, education, and science. Material influence is attested by numerous Sumerian loanwords in Akkadian, some of which were taken over by later Semitic dialects. Elamites and Persians, Hurrians, Hittites, and Urarteans, Phoenicians and Hebrews, all were among the direct or indirect heirs of Sumerian civilization. These facts have long been familiar. What is less common is the realization that the civilizing activity of the Sumerians had begun in proto-historic times; that the chief beneficiary of that activity was the social side of civilization; and that as a result of that activity the whole of Western Asia was to become a cultural unit, for all its heterogeneous and polyglot components which were to pass in review in the course of millennia. So strong was the assimilatory effect of the framework which the Sumerians had left, that the Semites and non-Semites who were caught in it came to have more in common than did the Semites and the Egyptians, in spite of the linguistic ties that bound the two latter groups.[36]

Space will not permit to furnish detailed support for these assertions. Only the general line of reasoning can be indicated at present. It starts with the emergence of writing at the end of the Uruk period.

Adam Falkenstein has demonstrated[37] that the earliest written records found in Sumer represent the absolute beginning of that script. Its direct predecessor was the cylinder seal, since many figures which occur on the oldest seals appear also on the earliest tablets. Writing first served the purposes of temple economy, with private business turning to the new medium shortly afterwards. Historical and literary compositions are the result of subsequent development. From the very beginning, however, lists of signs are compiled as a guide to the scribe and the reader. Now the cylinder seal is admittedly of Mesopotamian origin, hence the derivative script bespeaks the same source; this con-

[36] Hence the many close ties between the Hurrians and the Hebrews as against the less substantial cultural connection between the Hebrews and the neighboring Egyptians. The traditional opposition of the Hebrews to the Egyptians may indeed be viewed in the same light.

[37] *Archaische Texte aus Uruk.*

clusion is borne out by independent considerations.[38] Finally, the language used in the texts of the Jemdet Nasr period is demonstrably Sumerian. Since the first tablets are only slightly older, and since they are all but identical with those of the Jemdet Nasr age, they can scarcely represent any other language. The introduction of writing was therefore the work of the Sumerians.

Let us now carry this demonstration to its logical conclusion. Writing was not a deliberate invention, but the incidental by-product of a strong sense of private property, always a characteristic of classical Sumerian civilization. The cylinder seal was a device to identify owners of goods, presented to the temple or the object of private transactions, and the first tablets merely implement the operation of temple economy. The same respect for private property is reflected in the records of purchases made by later rulers of Sumer and Akkad;[39] it is epitomized in the fundamental tenet of the Code of Hammurabi that a purchase not accompanied by a written document is a theft punishable by death;[40] and it is exhaustively illustrated by the tens of thousands of business documents recovered from the archives of ancient Mesopotamia.

Sumerian government and governmental economy reveal the same basic orientation. The Sumerian city state represents a commercial theocracy in which private enterprise had an important place. The pronounced legalistic order finds its expression in collections of laws which are to become paradigmatic for Babylonia, Assyria, Anatolia, and Palestine, and are implicit in the legal documents of the Elamites, the Kassites, and the Hurrians. The legal framework is transplanted by means of the cuneiform writing,[41] itself an early offshoot of Sumerian economy. In-

[38] Based on the inner evidence of the script; cf. *ibid*. 25–6. For the bearing of the cylinder seals see also Frankfort, *Cylinder Seals* 1.

[39] Cf. e.g., Urukagina, Cones B and C, cols. xi–xii. [See now the article of B. A. van Proosdij in the Koschaker Festschrift (*Studia et Documenta* II; Leiden, 1939) 235 ff.]

[40] § 7; cf. M. Schorr, *Vorderasiatische Bibliothek* 5 (1913) xiii.

[41] It is worthy of notice that the Hurrian and Hittite syllabaries rest on a prototype which antedates the Dynasty of Hammurabi; cf. JAOS 58. 189, note 68.

evitably, religious and literary elements are transmitted with the legal ideas. Sumero-Akkadian deities are given a place in the Hurrian pantheon,[42] and the Epic of Gilgamesh is translated into Hurrian and Hittite. In this manner, Sumerian writing, bearing the fruits of Sumerian civilization, pervades the whole of Western Asia, thus achieving a more lasting and far-reaching effect than the most extensive conquests of Mesopotamian emperors. Babylonian kings struggle to phrase their accounts in a language already dead.[43] Remote Ugarit uses that language in its vocabularies. Ashurbanipal boasts of his ability to read inscriptions in the "obscure Sumerian,"[44] and Achaemenian kings employ formulaic phrases which echo statements by Sumerian rulers. But it is always the law, the *torah* in the language of a culturally related center, that governs human conduct and safeguards human progress.

This sketch is not intended to minimize non-Sumerian contributions to the civilization of Western Asia. But too much emphasis cannot be placed on the original Sumerian nucleus. In the course of millennia it was modified, improved, and adjusted to various local requirements. Notable additions to it were made. But the basic legal, administrative, and scientific elements can be traced to the early days of the emergence and evolution of writing. Those elements remain operative as late as Persian and classical times.

The one section of the ancient East that was not involved in this course of social progress was Egypt. The determining factor may be traced to the secondary position of the law in the Egyptian social order. This position was determined in turn by a radically different concept of the rights of the individual. The king was here the supreme judge and the ultimate master of all he surveyed. His was an authoritarian state that knew no higher power. Hence Egyptian government and Egyptian law follow

[42] See A. Götze, *Kleinasien* (1933) 125.

[43] Cf. A. Poebel, *AfO* 9 (1933–4). 50–1. The influence of Sumerian on the "classical" dialect of Hammurabi Akkadian is stronger than is generally recognized. A good illustration is furnished by the *t*-form of Akkadian as interpreted by Goetze, JAOS 56.333.

[44] Cf. B. Meissner, *Babylonien und Assyrien* 2.328.

a pattern of their own, and that pattern is not upset until Assyrian and Persian conquests have drawn Egypt into the orbit of the West Asiatic civilization.

III. THE UNDERLYING ETHNIC ELEMENTS

It is evident from our consideration of the material remains left by the early inhabitants of Mesopotamia that many ethnic elements contributed to the final product which is handed over to the people of the Early Dynastic times. Common survivals, cross-fertilization, and diffusion may have contributed to the leveling of such cultures as those of the Halaf and Obeid periods; but geographical differences alone would have been sufficient to differentiate in course of time the underlying ethnic groups.[45] Subsequent changes in the course of the Uruk period herald the arrival of fresh ethnic elements, and the same is true of the Jemdet Nasr period. That a degree of continuity is preserved, nevertheless, is due mainly to the way in which early civilization advanced. Fresh arrivals may have aided in the progress of the invaded areas. They were in a position to improve, but could not entirely obliterate, the cumulative and synthesized heritage of the past.

To identify the individual ethnic elements which cooperated in producing the civilization of preliterate Mesopotamia is a more hopeless task today than it ever appeared to be. It did not seem nearly as difficult before we found out that the culture of each period was a composite fabric. Furthermore, physical anthropology held out the hope that the racial strains might be disentangled. But this promise has not been fulfilled. In fact, the available anthropometric evidence is less conclusive in this respect than the circumstantial evidence from material remains.[46] The process of racial leveling is immeasurably older than that

[45] Note, e.g., the individualizing elements in Susa I, the Nineveh area, and Lower Mesopotamia in Obeid times which tend to break down the underlying cultural relationship of these three regions.

[46] See the monograph of W. M. Krogman in *Or. Inst. Pub.* xxx (1937) 213–85.

of cultural blending. The latter process did not succeed in obliterating all heterogeneous elements, and the chronological testimony of stratigraphy enables us to recognize an intrusive group even where the skeletal evidence may be non-committal.

When we work back from historic times, we encounter the Sumerians at the end of the Uruk period. The question that comes up next is whether the Sumerians had been in the land from the time of the earliest settlements, or arrived in any one of the succeeding stages. This question is not a new one. There is, however, new evidence that bids fair to bring it nearer to a satisfactory solution. Only a bare outline of the relevant facts can be given at this time.

The arrival of the Sumerians at the beginning of the Obeid period has been advocated most energetically by Frankfort.[47] He bases his conclusion on the argument from continuity, although he is aware that the continuity which he seeks to establish is broken in many significant points. Mesopotamian pottery, for example, is kaleidoscopic in its succession of distinctive families.

Not to repeat the arguments for a later arrival of the Sumerians which I have given in full on other occasions,[48] I shall make only the following additions. The Sumerians are definitely in Lower Mesopotamia in the latter half of the Uruk period, when the cylinder seals and writing first appear. Now Uruk B is characterized also by significant changes in pottery and architecture and the appearance of a pronounced naturalistic style in sculpture, a style which dominates, furthermore, the contemporary glyptic art. Now these changes, and particularly the abandonment of the earlier stamp seal, are radical enough to betray the intrusion of a forceful and heterogeneous ethnic group. The most logical candidates for that event are the Sumerians.

But we can go further than that. Now that Lower Mesopotamia is matched and exceeded in antiquity by the north, we have there a reliable contemporary witness. If the Obeid period in Lower Mesopotamia was of Sumerian origin, then its northern

---

[47] *Archaeology and the Sumerian Problem* 40 ff.
[48] AJA 37 (1933). 459 ff.

counterpart must have been Sumerian, too. And yet there is nothing in the mass of contemporary material from Gawra and Arpachiya that might foreshadow the typically Sumerian products of a later date. The human representations of the period are unlike anything achieved by the Sumerians. Most important of all are the seals, of which we have now a large collection. Not only are the northern seals of the Obeid period stamps and not cylinders, but their style is also radically different from the style of the second phase of Uruk. It is linear and schematized, not full-bodied and naturalistic.[49] Naturalistic style, cylinder seals, and writing are unmistakable witnesses of Sumerian occupation. None of these witnesses appears in the north before Jemdet Nasr times, when the earlier direction of cultural diffusion from north to south is reversed. In short, Sumerian presence is not felt in the north in any of the periods prior to Jemdet Nasr. Since there was a close relationship between north and south in Obeid times, the Sumerians cannot have been the authors of that age. Other cultures flourished before their arrival, and it is to those cultures, as we have seen, that the country owed a degree of continuity.[50]

[49] The stamp seals from Gawra VII-VIII, published in my *Excavations at Tepe Gawra I* (1935) pls. lvi–viii, can now be supplemented by a large number of seals and impressions from the earlier levels. Their cumulative evidence is to the effect that nothing comparable in style to the seals from Uruk IV and later is present at Gawra until the very end of the Uruk period. In other words, the glyptic style that is characteristic of the Sumerians does not begin to affect the north until the Sumerians had demonstrable contacts with the south.

[50] Frankfort's argument that the Sumerians were "the earliest occupants of the valley of the Two Rivers" rests on the premise "that the continuity in the material culture of Mesopotamia may best be understood as based on a similar ethnic continuity which, in view of the later stages of the development, we have to call from the very beginning Sumerian" (op. cit. 46). The first part of this proposition is self-evident: ethnic survivals as transmitters of material accomplishments may safely be assumed from the beginning of chalcolithic times at least. But the conclusion does not follow at all. One could say with equal right that the Hurrians of the Kirkuk area were its original population because the texts of the second millennium use the script and reflect many legal and administrative ideas of the preceding millennium. What is characteristically Sumerian in Lower Mesopotamia turns out to strain the normal continuity instead of maintaining it. The underlying influences are eccentric rather than concentric.

(*cont'd*)

All signs point, therefore, to the arrival of the Sumerians in the course of the Uruk period, and no real difficulty is occasioned by this assumption.

It follows that the foundations of the historic civilization of Mesopotamia were laid in Uruk times. The next stage was one of intensive coordination and readjustment. Increasing wealth brought in new elements, specifically from Elam and the west. But the Sumerian framework had been established and was gaining strength. Presently it was ready for emergence into the Early Dynastic order and the full light of history.

Thus ended the second phase of the Sumerian Problem. World War II interrupted archaeological excavation, and many scholars found themselves engrossed with problems more current than the Sumerian one. In the postwar years, as we shall see, the question was revived as new finds and new ideas gave it a different aspect.

The Sumerians were later arrivals, therefore, who injected new and vital elements into the inherited civilization.

PART THREE
The Third Phase: New Approaches and a Rationalization

Whatever hope anyone might have had that the Sumerian Problem had been laid to rest was rudely dashed by the report of the new excavations at Eridu (1948), the disturbing linguistic suggestions of the great Benno Landsberger (1943–45), and the novel approach through comparative literature offered by Samuel Noah Kramer (1948). The new state of affairs in 1951 was admirably summarized by Speiser:[1]

I

The Sumerians played a decisive part in the formation and development of the historic civilization of Mesopotamia. Their tangible influence on the region's law and society, religion and literature, and its arts and sciences persisted well into the Hellenistic age, although the last Sumerian state had become but a dim memory as early as the days of Hammurabi. Moreover the introduction of writing by the Sumerians ushered in the recorded history of mankind as a whole. Lastly, the vitality of the composite Sumero-Akkadian civilization is attested not only by its spread in antiquity beyond the confines of Mesopotamia, but also by its tenaciousness in the later Near East and its sundry survivals in the West, down to our own times. The

---

[1] E. A. Speiser, "The Sumerian Problem Reviewed," *Hebrew Union College Annual*, **23** Part One (1950–1), pp. 339–355. Reprinted by permission of the Hebrew Union College Annual.

Sumerians, in short, may be said to have made history in more ways than one.[2]

The problem of Sumerian origins is thus of more than strictly local and temporary interest. It is rather a question concerning a pioneering element in the evolution of civilization in general. But because history proper was made possible by the Sumerians, and because Sumerian beginnings go back of necessity to prehistoric times, the problem of these beginnings in prehistory cannot be solved by the direct evidence of historic data alone. We have to fall back for much of our material on the circumstantial testimony of inarticulate sources. The pertinent material is diversified, unwieldy, and often inconclusive. Some of the basic details are still missing and quite possibly may never be recovered. Any proposed reconstruction of the underlying pattern will be subject, therefore, to the customary test of a working hypothesis: how comprehensive and efficient is the suggested solution?

The whole problem of Sumerian origins is of relatively recent date. In the days when the First Dynasty of Ur was still thought to be legendary—a scarce thirty years ago—Sumerians and Semites were generally regarded as the only significant factors in the early history and prehistory of Lower Mesopotamia. Furthermore, since Sumerian records antedated Akkadian sources, this precedence was usually viewed as an index of absolute origins. With the rapid progress, however, of archaeological investigations in the nineteen-twenties there came a corresponding broadening of horizons and deepening of insight. Early literary documents could be coordinated for the first time with carefully analyzed stratigraphic evidence, thus leading to a proper appreciation of the great depth and complexity of the antecedent preliterate occupations. And as additional cultures came to light, each with its own peculiar geographic and chronological features, the larger issue of origins and interrelations could no longer be restricted to

[2] Cf. *Studies in the History of Culture* (in honor of Waldo G. Leland). 1942, pp. 55 ff. Attention may be called also to the general summary in my *The United States and the Near East* (1947, 1950), 28 ff.

Sumerians and Semites.[3] Accordingly, Sumerian beginnings emerged as a complex and many-sided problem.

Within the past twenty years the proposed interpretations of this problem have followed one of two main lines of approach: (a) The Sumerians were not the first in the land, having arrived in Lower Mesopotamia after the foundation of its earliest culture, but before the start of the first historic age. (b) The Sumerians were themselves the founders of the earliest prehistoric culture of Lower Mesopotamia—historic Sumer—and were hence the authors of the so-called el-Obeid stage. The first of these theories has been traced back at times to my *Mesopotamian Origins* (1930).[4] While this ascription is not strictly correct,[5] it is true that when my formulation was attempted it was possible to make far more extensive use of the combined archaeologic-epigraphic evidence than had been the case previously, so that a fuller and broader analysis could hardly be avoided. On the other hand, the alternative view of absolute Sumerian priority has been sponsored consistently by Professor Henri Frankfort, who first expressed it with all his usual persuasiveness and penetration in a monograph entitled *Archaeology and the Sumerian Problem* (1932).[6]

Since the appearance of these two studies various writers have indicated preference for the one position or the other. The current division would seem to be in doubt. Seton Lloyd, for instance, writing in 1947, declared: "In the years which followed, Speiser's conclusion, though not his reasoning, came to be increasingly favoured."[7] But Father R. T. O'Callaghan,

---

[3] For an important sidelight on this question see Th. Jacobsen, "The Assumed Conflict Between Sumerians and Semites in Early Mesopotamian History," *JAOS* 59 (1939), 485 ff.

[4] Abbreviated henceforth as *MO*.

[5] Painted pottery in the south had caused R. C. Thompson to assume a pre-Sumerian ethnic element as early as 1920; cf. *Archaeologia* LXX, 109 ff.; and the non-Sumerian character of the oldest place names was mentioned in passing by B. Meissner, *AfO* V (1929), 8.

[6] *Studies in Ancient Oriental Civilizations*, No 4 (Chicago Oriental Institute); abbreviated *ASP*.

[7] *Sumer* III, 92.

writing a few months later (1948), stated: "This stand [referring to the same conclusion] is rejected by most scholars."[8] At least one of the statistical estimates obviously must be wrong. Nor is the truth of the matter of any particular significance. The only pertinent question is whether the total available evidence justifies as yet a definite preference either way. Neither Frankfort's formulation nor mine could be reprinted today without very extensive modifications in detail. Much new material has come to light in the meantime, and older sources have been re-examined in several notable instances. The whole Sumerian problem merits, therefore, a comprehensive review in the form of a brief situation report.

II

The main areas of potential information on the question before us may be analyzed as follows:

1. Linguistically, the structure of Sumerian stands out today with unusual clarity and transparent inner logic, for all that countless minor details remain to be worked out.[9] The literary treasures of the Sumerians are steadily adding to our knowledge and appreciation of mankind's early historic progress. Nevertheless, all efforts to link Sumerian to some larger linguistic stock have failed thus far, although such efforts have ranged all the way from Central Africa to East Asia and Oceania.[10] This line of inquiry, therefore, promises no direct answer to the question regarding the original home of the Sumerians. The negative results obtained to date can have only an indirect and circumstantial bearing.

[8] *Aram Naharaim* (Analecta Orientalia 26), 12, note 1.

[9] The highly advanced status of Sumerian grammatical studies today may be judged from A. Falkenstein's *Grammatik der Sprache Gudeas von Lagas*, I (Analecta Orientalia 28), 1949.

[10] Cf. V. Christian's *Die sprachliche Stellung des Sumerischen, Babyloniaca* XII, fascs. 3–4 (1943). The author concludes that Sumerian resulted from a mixture of a relatively pure type of Caucasic with an earlier blend of Hamitic and Asiatic-Sudanese (p. 125)—a theory which speaks for itself. Note also Karl Bouda, *Die Beziehungen des Sumerischen zum Baskischen, Westkaukasischen und Tibetischen, MAOG* XII/3 (1938).

2. Anthropometrically, the evidence is ambiguous and confused. The number of crania examined is as yet very small, relatively speaking, especially when the prodigious time span involved is taken into consideration. The consensus would seem to be, with all the necessary reservations, that the basic population of the whole region consisted of Mediterranean longheads, who were joined in course of time and relatively late by several groups of Alpine roundheads.[11] Both these physical types, of course, could have been represented by more than one linguistic stock. In this connection it should be stressed that there is a marked discrepancy between the evidence of the cemeteries uncovered in Sumer and the appearance of the historic Sumerians as depicted on the monuments. For it has been repeatedly observed that the monumental representations of the Sumerians point for the most part to pronounced roundheads.[12]

3. Archaeologically, the evidence has been growing steadily in volume and in complexity. Prior to the first historic age in Mesopotamia we can now distinguish a long succession of distinctive strata which—for Mesopotamia as a whole—add up to some thirty separate occupational levels. These levels fall into several individual cultural units. In the south, which includes Sumer proper, we find, starting with the latest of these protohistoric cultures and, moving back into the past, the following major groups:[13] (a) The so-called "Protoliterate,"[14]

---

[11] Cf. W. M. Krogman's study in H. H. von der Osten's *The Alishar Hüyük* III (1937), pp. 213 ff., especially 269 ff. To the full bibliography which this monograph contains may now be added R. J. Braidwood's "Asiatic Prehistory and the Origin of Man," *JNES* VI (1947), 30 ff., for purposes of broader orientation. Charlotte M. Otten, in her preliminary study of the skeletal material from the Obeid cemetery at Eridu (*Sumer* IV, 1948, 125 ff.,), concludes (p. 125): "This is unquestionably a Caucasoid population."

[12] A. Moortgat, *Die Entstehung der sumerischen Hochkultur* (Der Alte Orient 43, 1945), 60.

[13] For purposes of ready reference, the terminology here followed is that used in Ann Louise Perkins' comprehensive study, *The Comparative Archaeology of Early Mesopotamia* (Studies in Ancient Oriental Civilization, No. 25), 1949.

[14] An unsatisfactory designation, to my thinking, in that it really begs the question.

corresponding roughly to what used to be called "Jemdet Nasr." (b) "Uruk" or "Warka." (c) "Obeid" or "Ubaid." Until the recent discoveries at Eridu it was thought that the oldest Obeid levels marked the beginning of stratigraphically attested occupations in Sumer. The discovery, however, of (c') the "Eridu" ware poses a new problem which will be touched upon later.

The above groups have their counterparts in the north which can be correlated chronologically with their respective southern analogues and show in addition a number of important material links. Because of its greater geologic antiquity, however, the north has proved to contain major cultural centers antedating the oldest known from the south. Thus it has yielded multiple levels of (d) the "Halaf" culture which underly the oldest northern analogues of Obeid. Moreover, we have now a series of (e) "Hassunah" deposits anterior to Halaf. Finally, there are abundant witnesses of yet another culture which has come to be known under the name of (e') "Samarra." Where its stratification and classification have been established beyond all doubt, Samarra has been found to co-exist with the later phases of Hassunah; for instance, at the site of Hassunah itself.[15] For the purpose of the present review it will suffice to note the presence of Samarra and its approximate chronologic place without giving it an independent listing.

How many separate ethnic-cultural groups does this archaeological evidence oblige us to assume? There are enough ties between the Protoliterate stage (a) and the earliest historic Sumerians to warrant our positing of an underlying ethnic link. This would still leave us, however, with five major cultural groups (b-e) before the Protoliterate period, if Mesopotamia as a whole is to be considered, as it properly must be. There is, to be sure, the possibility that more than one ethnic element participated in the evolution of a single distinctive prehistoric

[15] Cf. R. J. Braidwood, *JNES* IV (1945), 261. For the characteristics of the cultural stages just listed see the studies of Perkins and Moortgat mentioned above, and add André Parrot, *Archéologie mésopotamienne* (1946).

culture. Conversely, the same ethnic group may have had a part in the development of more than one culture. Furthermore, the absolute culture individuality of Eridu and Samarra (c', e') may be open to doubt for one reason or another; this is why neither has been given an independent listing, so as not to prejudge the issue. Nevertheless, it would be extremely hazardous to argue, in the face of the mass of cumulative evidence available to us, that Uruk, Obeid, Halaf, and Hassunah, or any smaller combination of these units, went back ultimately to a single ethnic strain. All our evidence would seem to point to the conclusion that the prehistoric composition of Mesopotamia was as complex ethnically as it was culturally.

4. Geographically, the historic Sumerians are first seen concentrated at the head of the Persian Gulf, whence they advance gradually up the Tigris-Euphrates valley. Their script and their cylinder seals are the tracers that enable us to follow the spread of Sumerian civilization, or of sundry elements thereof, to the shores of the Mediterranean and beyond. Yet the Sumerians themselves were never entrenched past the confines of Lower Mesopotamia. This rigid geographic limitation contributes an argument whose significance has all too often been entirely overlooked.

5. Lastly, due weight must be given to the combined linguistic-geographic testimony of the place names. It is certainly very suggestive that nearly all, if not all, of the known oldest cities of Sumer have proved to bear non-Sumerian names. In fact, it was this particular onomastic feature that led me, twenty years ago, to probe more extensively into the whole question of Sumerian origins.[16] Since the very prominence and antiquity of the cities involved pointed to the logical conclusion that non-Sumerian meant in this case pre-Sumerian, the further assumption was in order that we were faced here with a pre-Sumerian linguistic substratum. With this premise as a starting point, the other lines of investigation appeared to yield readily a consistent pattern. The isolated character of Sumerian could

---

[16] *MO*, 26 ff. Cf. also the supplementary remarks in *AJA* 37 (1933), 459 ff., and *JAOS* 59 (1939), Supplement, 17 ff.

be explained by the intrusion of its speakers into an area in which totally different stocks had long been at home. Round-heads arriving from a considerable distance, and hence presumably in relatively small numbers, would not alter drastically the prevailing ratio of longheads. Since the Obeid culture and its analogues occupied vast areas of the ancient Near East and appeared to be autochthonous in that general neighborhood, the sharp geographic restriction of the Sumerian centers called for a correlation with a culture that was far less extensive than the Obeid. The Uruk culture, or a sub-phase of it, answered these requirements. All in all, the combined evidence of all the major sources of potential information—as they were known and understood at the time—seemed to favor the conclusion that the Sumerians were not the first settlers in Lower Mesopotamia. Their arrival, accordingly, would have to be placed after the Obeid occupation, and hence in the Uruk period.[17]

When Frankfort, nevertheless, came out two years later in favor of Sumerian priority, he did not attempt to refute the opposing argument point by point. The onomastic results could not be ignored, but Frankfort countered with the suggestion that non-Sumerian was not necessarily synonymous in this case with pre-Sumerian. The cities in question might have borne Sumerian names originally, only to have their names changed at some period when the basic population was temporarily overshadowed by heterogeneous ethnic elements.[18] This would imply, however, something like the following sequence of events: The Sumerians establish the Obeid civilization and found the cities which are destined to maintain their importance far into the historic peroid. A foreign group supplants the Sumerians and renames their major centers. The Sumerians eventually throw off the foreign yoke and recapture their cities—but they

[17] The Protoliterate period is too late since it has yielded many typically Sumerian features.

[18] Lest these critical remarks be misunderstood, it may be in order to emphasize that the advantage of hindsight is likely to place earlier opinions in an unfavorable light which they by no means merit. The steadily increasing debt under which Frankfort has placed all students of the ancient Near East is too obvious to require stressing.

retain the alien place-names, even though it is precisely these
very centers that come to symbolize Sumerian culture and
political authority. The explanation, in short, is highly improbable.

The heart of Frankfort's thesis, however, is its archaeological
argument. It is this part of his presentation that has rightly
attracted most serious attention. Frankfort regarded as decisive
the existing evidence for cultural continuity from the Obeid
period on, as exemplified by recurring points of similarity
which link the earliest age with its several successors; most
especially in the physical type of the inhabitants, their dress,
and their hair styles. These features would outweigh, in Frankfort's view, the parallel evidence for discontinuity, best observed
in the drastic break in pottery styles which signalizes the end
of the Obeid and the beginning of the Uruk stages. In other
words, the archaeological side of the Sumerian problem would
narrow down to an emphasis on the legato theme in cultural
progress by the one side, and on the staccato theme by the
other.

Frankfort's thoughtful thesis left admittedly a number of
questions unanswered. Among these may be mentioned the
following: (a) How definite was the similarity of the material
features compared? (b) Was the weight of that argument sufficient to offset the undisputed evidence for a sharp break in
continuity which attended the termination of the Obeid period?
(c) Most important of all, could a working hypothesis be set
up without due regard to the other elements in the dispute,
namely: the linguistic isolation of Sumerian; the anthropometric disparity between the typical Sumerians of the monuments
and the people in the cemeteries of Sumer; the vast expanse
of the Obeid culture as contrasted with the sharply limited
spread of the known Sumerians; and the un-Sumerian names
of the oldest cities in Sumer? All these were weighty obstacles
to a ready acceptance of Frankfort's theory of Sumerian
priority. Nevertheless, the. opposing view likewise contained
enough uncertainties to cause the whole dispute to remain hung
up for some time.

III

The first scholar to revive the issue was Benno Landsberger. In a series of three articles, which appeared between 1943 and 1945,[19] Landsberger concentrated on the problem of a pre-Sumerian linguistic substratum to which I had already devoted considerable attention a dozen years earlier. He was able, however, to evoke from his sources an incomparably greater amount of suggestive material than had been the case hitherto. Not only could pre-Sumerian names be isolated, to Landsberger's discernment, from comparable Sumerian elements, but significant elements were seen by him likewise to follow a similar division. The substratum was thus credited with the basic vocabulary for farming, gardening, brewing, pottery, leather work, and building. To the Sumerians, on the other hand, have been assigned, by the same methodical procedure, the terms involving shipping, cattle feeding, jewelry, sculpture, glyptics, land measurement, writing, education, and law. Sumerian economy and society could thus be demarcated with a considerable show of reason from their earlier counterparts.[20] Sumerian thinking is seen to reflect a neatly ordered synthesis between things celestial and things terrestrial, tangibly sybolized by the ziggurat and the temple at its summit, a visible link between heaven and earth, between nature and society.[21] Landsberger's conclusion is that the Sumerians first appeared at the end of the Obeid period, having arrived by sea from a considerable distance—a conclusion that is thus in detailed and gratifying accord with my earlier assumptions, which were based in large part on entirely different arguments.

Anton Moortgat's monograph, *Die Entstehung der sume-*

[19] *Ankara Fakültesi Dergisi:* (a) I (1943), 97-102; (b) II (1944), 431-38; (c) III (1945), 150-59.

[20] Ibid. (b). Landsberger distinguishes in fact two distinct substrata. The full import of these studies, however, cannot be properly evaluated so long as the detailed presentation remains unpublished.

[21] Ibid. (c).

rischen Hochkultur (1945),[22] analyzes the over-all archaeological yield from the several prehistoric periods of Western Asia. He, too, feels obliged to sort out the manifestly Sumerian from the indigenous. As undisputed Sumerian contributions Moortgat names the cycle of the mother goddess and the fertility god, and the ziggurat surmounted by a temple. In this last-named ascription in particular Moortgat is in full agreement with Landsberger, although each worked with sources not utilized by the other. While admitting the complexity of the problem as a whole, Moortgat is inclined to date the arrival of the Sumerians in the Uruk period, without in any way pressing this conclusion.[23]

S. N. Kramer's approach to the problem of Sumerian origins is strictly unique.[24] He proceeds from a consideration of the Sumerian Heroic Age in the light of other such ages in world literature. The heroic age, he argues, presupposes a superior underlying civilization which had attracted in course of time a people of primitive culture but endowed with youthful vigor and mobility. The invaders in the present instance were the Sumerians, who gradually gained the upper hand. Their arrival is dated to the period of transition between Obeid and Uruk. The nature of Kramer's argument is such that it can neither be proved nor disproved as a whole, although many of its details are admittedly vulnerable and capable of a clearer correlation with the known archaeological data. It may not be wholly gratuitous, however, to add in this connection that this theory is the product of an intimate student of Sumerian thought and that it has, at a minimum, the merit of a fresh and independent viewpoint.

The highly specialized subject of ancient Mesopotamian numeration may be in a position to shed some incidental light on the problem under discussion. In a recent article on the sexagesimal system. Dr. Hildegard Lewy arrived at the conclu-

[22] Cf. above, note 12.

[23] Op. cit., 94. See also the review by A. Falkenstein in *Bibliotheca Orientalis* V (1948), 93 f.

[24] Cf. his "New Light on the Early History of the Ancient Near East," *AJA* 52 (1948), 156 ff.

sion that "the entire development leading from the decimal to
the sexagesimal system was an accomplished fact when the
Sumerian numerals were named."[25] This would seem to constitute yet another link in the lengthening chain of cumulative
evidence which points to substantial cultural progress prior to
the arrival of the Sumerians, thus rendering that much less
probable the thesis of absolute Sumerian priority.

As against this manysided agreement about the relative
lateness of Sumerians in Lower Mesopotamia, there is one
contrary recent opinion based on evidence not hitherto adduced.
This evidence stems from the latest Iraqi excavations at Eridu.
Seton Lloyd's first account on the subject, published in 1947,
stressed the discovery of a group of temples from Levels VIII-
VI, dated to the Obeid period.[26] Their ground plan agrees with
one from Gawra XIII,[27] likewise of Obeid date, and foreshad-
ows the plans of the admittedly Sumerian temples from the
Protoliterate period at Warka. This architectural continuity,
Lloyd asserted, offsets the existing instances of discontinuity
and becomes decisive in confirming Frankfort's thesis that the
Sumerians were the founders of the Obeid culture and the
first settlers in the land.[28]

However, this sole new prop of the principle of continuity
collapsed with the very next campaign at Eridu. For below
the Obeid desposits there turned up several layers of an earlier
culture, the so-called Eridu phase, which is characterized in
particular by a novel ware. It was Lloyd himself who said
about the painted ornament on this Eridu ware that it presents
"elements reminiscent both of Tell Halaf and of Samarra,

---

[25] *JAOS* 69 (1949), 11.

[26] *Sumer* III (1947), 91 ff.

[27] Until the second volume of *The Excavations at Tepe Gawra* (by Mr.
A. J. Tobler), which went to the printers three years ago, is published, the
reader must be referred to my field account in *BASOR* 66 (1937), 2 ff.,
with the plan on p. 5.

[28] Cf. note 26 above. Lloyd's assertion (ibid. p. 91) that my "contrary
theory" was "largely based on philological evidence" would seem to leave
the curious impression that theories based on such evidence lack sufficient
validity. Besides, a considerable amount of archaeological evidence was
utilized by me in that connection.

although technically the ware does not in the least resemble either."[29] It would be premature to inquire at this early date into the precise relations of the Eridu culture, the oldest yet unearthed in Lower Mesopotamia. One is bound, however, to agree with the discoverers in maintaining the distinctiveness of Eridu as compared with Obeid. It would follow, then, that if the Sumerians were the founders of the Obeid culture, which succeeded Eridu, they can no longer be viewed as the earliest settlers in that area. That more than one cultural phase preceded the northern counterpart of Obeid, and that there could there-fore be no question of Sumerian priority in the north—even if the Sumerian authorship of the Obeid phase be granted for the sake of the argument—has been abundantly clear for a number of years.

IV

The chronologic angle of the Sumerian problem has thus been greatly simplified. Since no one would place the Sumerians in the land prior to Obeid proper, and since that cultural phase is not the first in the south—let alone in the north—the question that remains is whether Sumerian connections can plausibly be demonstrated for Obeid times, instead of being relegated to a later period. Let us first take up Lloyd's argument from architecture: namely, because the Protoliterate temples from Warka are Sumerian, and because they correspond to the Obeid temples from Eridu in ground plan, the Obeid builders were Sumerians. Of fundamental importance in this instance is the fact that the Sumerian ziggurat, which is present at Warka, is lacking both at Eridu[30] and at Gawra XIII. Moreover, we now have from the Obeid period not one temple plan, but three. There is the one to which Lloyd refers; it represents the round-the-corner, or lateral, type. Then there is the longitudinal type, the so-called *Langraum*, which we find in Gawra XI-XVIII,[31]

---

[29] *Sumer* IV (1948), 125.
[30] The ziggurat on that site belongs to a much later historic period.
[31] *The Smithsonian Report*, 1939, p. 443 and Pl. 7.2.

and which is destined to reassert itself in Gawra XI-VIII, and to become eventually characteristic of Assyria.[32] Lastly, there is the circular, or *tholos*, type, known from Gawra XVII and XX,[33] and from Halaf levels at nearby Arpachiyach. Surely, all three of these types were not Sumerian creations. In these circumstances it would seem to be logical to assume that the Sumerians adopted the design already established in the south, adding the temple tower as their own peculiar contribution. Lloyd's argument, at any rate, is no more cogent than would be some hypothetical assumption that because the mosque of Saint Sophia is Muslim, and because it was built under Justinian, therefore its builders must have been Muslims.

The argument from pottery has always militated against the thesis of Sumerian authorship of the Obeid culture. The painted pottery of the Obeid age is by far its most distinctive product. The succeeding Uruk wares are normally undecorated and otherwise different. Furthermore, if the Sumerians initiated the Obeid culture, they must have occupied at one time all of Mesopotamia, not to mention Iran and much of Baluchistan—in short, the known major centers of Obeid and its analogues. Yet at the beginning of the historic age the Sumerians are isolated in a small area at the head of the Persian Gulf. The regions formerly occupied by the Obeid folk are later inhabited by the demonstrably un-Sumerian Elamites, Lullu, Gutians, and others whose names have not been recorded. Elsewhere we find Semitic settlements and the early Hurrian sites. Amidst all this array of ethnic elements which are to remain familiar throughout the history of Mesopotamia—some of these down to our own times—the Sumerians are indeed a small, isolated, and disparate element. Clearly, it is not to their numbers that they owe their outstanding position in history.

No less indicative than the evidence of pottery is the testimony of the seals. Of the two general types, the stamp seal and the cylinder seal, the first one goes back to the Halaf period at least,[34] and becomes ubiquitous in Obeid times. In the Protoliter-

[32] See V. Müller, *JAOS* 60 (1940), 159.

[33] *The Smithsonian Report*, 1939, p. 443 and Pl. 8.1.

[34] That is to say, the earliest clearly stratified stamp seals belong to the

ate period the cylinder seal is introduced, to become the herald of the advancing Sumerian civilization. Where that civilization has made a mark, the stamp seal disappears; elsewhere, however, the stamps are retained. But when the syncretized Mesopotamian civilization is at long last brought to a close—late in the first millennium B.C.—the stamp returns from its prolonged retreat. Like the underlying physical type itself, the stamp seal had apparently been too firmly rooted to be driven out for ever by intrusive elements.

As regards the physical type, little store can be set by attempted reproductions prior to the historic age. With all due allowance, however, for the inadequacies of primitive techniques, it is scarcely possible to equate the prevailingly squat type of the known Sumerians with the narrow-waisted reproductions of earlier times; yet these reproductions are comparable among themselves, whether we find them in Obeid terracottas, engraved on Gawra stamps, or painted on the pottery from Susa. To go beyond such general characteristics and seek to detect from fragmentary reproductions in clay such minute details as beards and hair styles is unprofitable, to say the least. Parenthetically, we now know from the sculptured remains of the Protoliterate period that bearded and beardless types were common in Mesopotamia on the eve of the historic age,[35] and may be presumed to have played their respective parts long before that. Cultural complexity may be supposed to reflect a variety of underlying ethnic types; it will produce, at any rate, a diversity of concurrent fashions.

Correlations between cranial types and linguistic stocks can never merit much attention, except perhaps as footnotes to conclusions arrived at independently. At all events, the suggestion may be hazarded that the basic Mediterranean type of

---

Halaf age (at Gawra). It is not certain, however, whether the actual introduction of these seals is not to be pushed back sufficiently to allow for the necessary period of evolution.

[35] Cf., e.g., the figures on the alabaster vase from Warka, depicted and discussed by E. Heinrich, *Kleinfunde* (1936), pp. 15-17 and Pls. 2-3; Mrs. E. D. Van Buren, *AfO* XIII, 32 ff.; A. Moortgat, op. cit. 88 ff.; F. Basmachi, *Sumer* III (1947), 118 ff.

the region[36] belonged linguistically to Caucasoid and Semitic stocks. Alpine elements appear to have been intrusive. The Sumerians might well have been included among them. On the assumption that they were intruders among long-established and physically related local groups, the Sumerians would not affect appreciably the existing radical balance. Arrival from a considerable distance, especially if they had come by sea, would suggest relatively small numbers. Although they eventually became dominant—within the narrow confines of their settlement—in the political and social sense, they need not have pervaded all the strata of the population. Beyond the limits of southermost Mesopotamia the Sumerian physical type could scarcely have attained prominence in any case. If the skeletal material from a given Sumerian center of a historic period should show a predominance of longheads, while the sculptured figures from the same site show a majority of shortheads, this would be in entire accord with the assumption of a basic native population ruled by physically dissimilar invaders. Analogously, we should expect a future archaeologist excavating a Syrian site of the mid-twentieth century of our era to find ample evidence of Arab culture and Arabic records. But the skeletal remains would hardly conform to the classic Arab type.

To sum up, our present material bearing on the problem of Sumerian origins would appear to add up to this: The Sumerians arrived at the head of the Persian Gulf not earlier than the close of the Obeid period, coincident perhaps with the rise of the Uruk stage, or possibly even as its founders. They had come from the east, probably by sea, although their original home seems to have been in a highland zone. That home has to be sought beyond the Iranian province, for that is already pre-empted by others. It would be futile to speculate now—and the prospects do not seem bright for a more profitable attempt of this kind in the foreseeable future—whether that home was in Transcaucasia, Transcaspia, or somewhere in Farther Asia. The Sumerians came to dominate, but did not drive out, the earlier settlers. They took over many of the

---

[36] See above, note 11.

cultural gains of the past, while adding and developing significant features of their own. In some way which is beyond our means to determine, but not beyond our ability to appreciate, the resulting blend was to become an important factor in the history of all mankind.

If this sketch is approximately right, the Sumerian problem has been clarified in so far as the relative chronology of that people's appearance is concerned. But the question of the ultimate home of the Sumerians is no nearer a solution than it has ever been.

Two important matters discussed by Speiser require further elaboration: (1) the hypothesis of Kramer and (2) the finds at Eridu. We may begin by reproducing the Kramer article in full:[37]

One of the more significant problems in the early history of the Near East revolves about the arrival of the Sumerians in Mesopotamia. Briefly put, it may be stated as follows: Were the Sumerians the first people to settle in Lower Mesopotamia, or were they preceded there by one or more ethnic groups? To be sure, in the course of the past several decades, the prehistoric levels of a number of important Mesopotamian sites have been excavated to some extent, and a not inconsiderable quantity of early remains have been brought to light. Unfortunately these new finds have not resolved the "Sumerian problem"; indeed they have served to divide the Near Eastern archaeologists into two diametrically opposed camps. Since this may seem rather strange to scholars not specializing in Mesopotamian archaeology, it will be useful to summarize the facts, if only in the briefest outline.[38]

[37] S. N. Kramer, "New Light on the Early History of the Ancient Near East," *American Journal of Archaeology*, LII (1948), pp. 156–164. Reprinted by permission of the American Journal of Archaeology and the author.

[38] For lucid and basic statements of the problems involved, cf. Frankfort, *Archaeology and the Sumerian Problem* (*SAOC*, iv), and Speiser, *The Beginnings of Civilization in Mesopotamia* (*JAOS*, supplement 4). To the literature cited in note 1 of Speise'rs study, add now especially Andrae in Walter Otto's *Handbook der Archäologie*, pp. 643–678; McCown, *The Comparative Stratigraphy of Early Iran* (*SAOC*, xxiii); Delougaz and Lloyd, *Presargonid Temples in the Diyala Region* (*OIP*, lviii); Frankfort's

(cont'd)

The earliest cultural phase of Lower Mesopotamia is divided by general agreement in accordance with a number of pertinent archaeological criteria into two distinct periods, the Obeid period, the remains of which are always found immediately above virgin soil, and the Uruk period, the remains of which overlie those of the Obeid period. Moreover, and again by general agreement, the Uruk period itself is subdivided into two major stages, an earlier and a later. Now it is in the later stage of the Uruk period that we find the introduction of the cylinder seal as well as our first inscribed tablets. And since according to present indications the language represented on these tablets, in spite of the largely pictographic character of the signs, seems to be Sumerian, most archaeologists agree that the Sumerians must already have been in Lower Mesopotamia during the later stage of the Uruk period. It is with respect to the earlier part of the Uruk period and the still earlier Obeid period that we find a very serious conflict of views. From an analysis of the material remains of these earlier periods, the one group of archaeologists concludes that while their remains differ considerably from those of the later stage of the Uruk period, and of the periods which follow, they can nevertheless be recognized as the prototypes from which the latter developed, and since these latter are admittedly Sumerian, the earliest remains, too, must be attributed to the Sumerians; hence the Sumerians were the first settlers in Mesopotamia. On the other hand, another group of archaeologists, after analyzing practically identical archaeological data, arrives at an exactly opposite con-

---

"Introduction" to Lloyd and Safar's report on Tell Uqair (*JNES*, ii, pp. 131-134); Van der Meer, "The Al-Obeid Culture and Its Relation to the Uruk and Jemdet Nasr Periods" (*Jaarbericht no. 8 van het Vooraziatisch-Egyptisch Gezelschap Ex Oriente Lux*, pp. 708-721); Mallowan, *Excavations at Braq and Chagar Bazar* (*Iraq*, ix, part 1); Burton-Brown, *Studies in Third Millennium History*; Lloyd's "Introduction" to Fuad Safar's report on Eridu (*Sumer*, iii, no. 2, pp. 85-95); Van der Meer, *The Ancient Chronology of Western Asia and Egypt*.

The following abbreviations are used in addition to those appearing in *AJA*, li, pp. 348 ff.: *AS, Assyriological Studies; OECT, Oxford Edition of Cuneiform Texts; ZA, Zeitschrift für Assyriologie.*

clusion. For these claim that while the remains of the earliest periods do show certain similarities to those of the later and admittedly Sumerian periods, the differences between them are significant enough to indicate a major ethnic break between the later stage of the Uruk period and the preceding phases, and since the former is Sumerian, the latter must be attributed to a pre-Sumerian culture in Lower Mesopotamia; hence the Sumerians were not the first settlers in that region.

It is obvious from the preceding summary, brief as it is, that as a result of the unavoidably subjective interpretation of the material archaeological evidence leading to two diametrically opposed conclusions, the solution of the "Sumerian problem" has reached more or less of an impasse. The present paper presents new evidence to show that not only were the Sumerians not the first in the land, but that they were preceded there by a more civilized power of considerable magnitude. Fortunately enough this new evidence has nothing to do with the highly ambiguous material remains of prehistoric Mesopotamia; it is of a purely literary and historical character. Moreover, it permits a fresh insight into the role played by the Sumerians in the earlier history of Lower Mesopotamia and sheds no inconsiderable light on that of the Near East as a whole.

The realization of the existence of this literary evidence came about as follows. In preparation for what is hoped to be the second of the seven-volume series of *Studies in Sumerian Culture*,[39] several years have been spent by me piecing together and reconstructing the extant texts of the Sumerian epic tales. At present there are available about a hundred clay tablets and fragments inscribed with Sumerian epic poetry; almost all date from the first half of the second millennium B.C. The great majority of these documents were excavated by the University of Pennsylvania at Nippur some fifty years ago and are now located in the University Museum at Philadelphia and in the Museum of the Ancient Orient in Istanbul. From all these tablets and fragments, published and unpublished, it is now

---

[39] Cf. the preface to my *Sumerian Mythology*.

possible to piece together wholly or in part nine epic tales, the extant texts of which vary in length from a little over one hundred to more than six hundred lines. Two of these epic tales revolve about the hero Enmerkar; two concern the hero Lugalbanda; five center about the most famous of the three heroes, Gilgamesh. A preliminary sketch of their contents appeared in a study entitled "Heroes of Sumer: A New Heroic Age in World History and Literature" (*Proceedings of the American Philosophical Society*, vol. xc, no. 2, pp. 120–130);[40] the scientific editions, including autograph copies of the unpublished texts in the University Museum and in the Museum of the Ancient Orient, are now in the process of preparation.[41]

In the course of this concentrated work on the Sumerian epic tales, it became ever more clear that early in their history, the Sumerians had passed through a cultural stage now commonly known as a Heroic Age. This fact turned out to be quite revealing. For, once the existence of a Sumerian Heroic Age had been determined, it was possible to adduce its cultural pattern and historic background on analogy with such long known Heroic Ages as those of the Greek, Indian, and Teutonic peoples. The results of this comparative analysis, in turn, proved highly significant for the possible resolution of the "Sumerian problem," and permitted a reinterpretation of the earliest history of Mesopotamia which may prove closer to the truth than those suggested hitherto. Let us turn therefore to a brief analysis of the various Heroic Ages.

It is largely to the credit of the English scholar H. Munro Chadwick[42] that it is now generally realized that the so-called Heroic Ages which we come upon from time to time and from place to place in the history of civilization are not mere

---

[40] For a more recent sketch of the epic tale "Enmerkar and the Lord of Aratta," resulting from the copying of a twelve column tablet in the Museum of the Ancient Orient in the fall of 1946, cf. my "Interim Report of Work in the Museum at Istanbul" (*BASOR*, civ, pp. 8-12).

[41] Cf. for the present, *Gilgamesh and the Huluppu Tree* (*AS*, x), "The Death of Gilgamesh" (*BASOR*, xciv, pp. 2-12), and "Gilgamesh and the Land of the Living" (*JCS*, i, pp. 3-46).

[42] Cf. H. Munro Chadwick, *The Heroic Age*; H. Munro and N. Kirshaw Chadwick, *The Growth of Literature*.

figments of the literary imagination, but represent very real and very significant social phenomena. Thus, to take only three of the more ancient and better known examples, there is the Teutonic Heroic Age which dominated much of northern Europe from the fourth to the sixth century A.D.; the Greek Heroic Age which flourished on the mainland of Greece toward the very end of the second millennium B.C.,[43] and finally the Heroic Age of India which probably dates only a century or so later than that of Greece. These three Heroic Ages reveal a marked and significant resemblance in social structure, governmental organization, religious concepts, and aesthetic expression; it is obvious that they owe their origin and being to very similar social, political, and psychological factors. The Sumerian Heroic Age now being revealed in its epic literature probably had its *floruit* no later than the first quarter of the third millennium B.C. Although it therefore precedes by more than a millennium and a half even the oldest of the three Indo-European Heroic Ages, that of the Greeks, it follows with remarkable closeness the culture pattern typical for those long known epochs.

Now the most characteristic feature of all four of our Heroic Ages is this: they represent a rather barbarous[44] cul-

---

[43] It is to be noted that the statements made in this paper with regard to the Greek Heroic Age are based on Chadwick's conclusions. My colleague John Franklin Daniel informs me that Chadwick's view, that the Achaeans were the people who invaded Greece and destroyed the Mycenaean civilization in the twelfth century B.C., is not likely to meet with general acceptance among students of early Greece. Daniel prefers to attribute this invasion to the Dorians, and suggests that the Achaeans be identified with the people who invaded the Greek mainland at the beginning of the Middle Helladic period, *ca.* 2000 B.C. This alternative hypothesis would fit into Chadwick's pattern and furnishes an apt parallel to the Sumerian development described below. The newcomers of the Middle Helladic period soon came into contact with the older and richer Minoan civilization of Crete, which influenced them profoundly. Gathering strength on land and becoming a maritime power, probably under Minoan tutelage, the mainlanders had become serious rivals of the Minoans by the sixteenth century B.C., and had wrested control of the Aegean from Crete by the fourteenth century. The Heroic Age falls a century or two later, with the expedition against Troy placed in the early twelfth century.

[44] Barbaric, primitive, and civilized societies are differentiated by Chad-
(cont'd)

tural stage in the life of a people which has come far indeed
from the primitive but has not yet attained the maturity and
stability of a civilized society. Its dominant element is a rather
numerous military class which prefers the soldierly life to
agriculture and labor, and to whom the underlying bulk of the
population counts for very little. It is these knightly aristocrats
who have freed themselves from the tribal obligations and
ideas which govern the more primitive peoples. At the same
time they have developed no true national organization and are
inspired by little if any national feeling; their success and failure
depend upon the personal prowess of their leaders and kings
whom they follow readily into all sorts of adventurous under-
takings, but from whom they are ready to drift away if these
tend to turn too peaceful or to become ungenerous in their
rewards.

If now we analyze the genesis and growth of the three Indo-
European Heroic Ages—and here again it is Chadwick's work
which is fundamental—and then apply the results of this
analysis to the analogous Sumerian Heroic Age, we come upon
a group of data that are significant and revealing not alone for
the early history of Lower Mesopotamia but for that of the
ancient Near East as a whole. For the factors primarily re-

---

wick as follows: "By primitive we mean the conditions of a local community which is sufficient for itself and dependent upon its own resources,
whether it live by hunting or by cultivation of the earth. It may be wholly
independent, or it may be subject, or perhaps tributary, to some dominant
power—which itself may be barbarous or civilized, but no external relations
are necessary for its own sake. By civilized we mean the conditions of a
society which is dependent for its existence—for the maintenance of its
civilization—upon relations with the wide world. Barbaric society as we
understand it, lies between these two extremes. The local community is one
of a number of similar communities which are grouped together under a
king or political organization. Each community contains an element which
is in intimate and necessary relation with elements in other local communities. These elements are the more typically barbaric elements; sometimes
they form an upper class. External relations with other groups vary both
in character and degree, but are never entirely wanting. When external
relations become a permanent necessity and widespread, the result is what
we call civilization" (Chadwick, *The Growth of Literature*, iii, p. 728).

sponsible for the more characteristic features of the Greek, Indian, and Teutonic Heroic Ages are two. In the first place these Heroic Ages coincide with a period of national migrations, a Völkerwanderungszeit. Secondly—and this is by far the more significant factor—these peoples, that is, the Achaeans, the Aryas, and the Teutons, while still on a relatively primitive and tribal level, had come in contact with a civilized power in the process of disintegration. Particularly as mercenaries in the military service of this power during its struggle for survival we find them absorbing the military technique, and to a superficial extent, some of the cultural accomplishments of their far more civilized neighbor. It is when they finally break through the frontiers of this civilized empire and carve out kingdoms and principalities for themselves within its territory, amassing considerable wealth in the process, that they develop that rather adolescent and barbaric cultural stage known as a Heroic Age.

Thus to take as an example the Heroic Age the historical antecedents of which are best known, the Teutonic Heroic Age, we find in the first place that it coincided with a period of national migrations. But more significantly, for a number of centuries preceding their Heroic Age, the relatively primitive Teutonic peoples had come in contact with the far more civilized but ever weakening Roman Empire, and had been subjected to its cultural influences, particularly no doubt as hostages in its court and as mercenaries in its armies. By the fifth and sixth centuries A.D. these Teutonic peoples had succeeded in occupying most of the territories which had formerly been part of the Roman Empire, and these are the two centuries that mark the *floruit* of the Teutonic Heroic Age.

If now we assume that the factors responsible for the origin and development of the Sumerian Heroic Age were analogous to those responsible for the origin and development of the Greek, Indian, and Teutonic Heroic Ages—and there seems to be no reason to assume otherwise—we may conclude in the first place that it must have coincided with a period of national migrations. More important, the occupation of Lower Mesopotamia by the Sumerians, which gave birth to their Heroic Age, must have marked the culminating stage in a historical process which had begun several centuries earlier, when Lower Mesopotamia was still part of a power whose state of civilization was far more advanced than that of the Sumerians who were settled somewhere along its outer fringes. It is from this more civilized power that the relatively primitive Sumerians, no doubt largely as mercenaries in its military employ, had absorbed in the course of time some of the essentials of its military technique as well as some of its more superficial cultural attainments. Finally, the Sumerians succeeded in breaking through the frontiers of this power, occupying a considerable portion of its territory, and amassing considerable wealth in the process; it is this period which marks the *floruit* of their Heroic Age. In short, as a result of the determining of the existence of a Sumerian Heroic Age, we seem justified in drawing the very significant conclusion that the Sumerians were *not* the first settlers in Lower Mesopotamia. Indeed the Sumerians must actually have been preceded by a civilized power of some magnitude, certainly one that was far more advanced culturally than the Sumerians, who, at the time they superseded it, that is, in the centuries emmediately preceding the Sumerian Heroic Age, must still have been a primitive people. As for what is generally spoken of as "Sumerian" civilization, that civilization which played so predominant a role in the Ancient Near East, and whose influence persisted long after the Sumerians had ceased to exist as a political entity, it must be looked upon as the product of some five or six centuries of cultural activity *following* the immature and barbaric Sumerian Heroic Age. It resulted no doubt from a constructive application of the Sumerian genius to the material and spiritual heritage of the pre-Sumerian civilization in Southern Mesopotamia.

With this fresh insight into the cultural morphology of early Lower Mesopotamia, let us now attempt to reconstruct the major outlines of its history; in spite of its necessarily oversimplified character, this tentative and hypothetical reconstruction should prove of considerable value for the interpretation and integration of the relevant archaeological material already unearthed in Southern Mesopotamia as well as of that still to be unearthed. From the days of the first settlements to those of the great

Accadian king Sargon, who may be said to mark the end of Sumerian political domination in the land, the history of Lower Mesopotamia may be divided into two major periods, the pre-Sumerian, which, as will soon become evident, may perhaps be more positively named the Irano-Semitic,[45] and the Sumerian.

The pre-Sumerian period began as a peasant-village culture; as is now generally agreed, it was introduced into Lower Mesopotamia by immigrants from southwestern Iran, noted particularly for their specialized type of painted pottery.[46] Not long after the establishment of the first settlement by the Iranian immigrants, the Semites probably infiltrated into Southern Mesopotamia both as peaceful immigrants and as warlike conquerors. It is probably largely as a result of the fusion of these two ethnic groups, the Iranians from the east and the Semites from the west, and the consequent cross-fertilization of their cultures, that there came into being the first civilized *urban* state in Lower Mesopotamia. As in the case of the later Sumerian civilization, it consisted of a group of city states between which there was continual strife for supremacy over the land as a whole. But now and again through the centuries relative unity and stability were no doubt achieved, at least for a brief interval. At such times, this Mesopotamian power, in which the Semitic element was no doubt predominant, must have succeeded in extending its influence over many of the surrounding districts, and developed what may well have been the first empire in the Near East, perhaps even the first empire in the history of civilization. Part of the territory which this empire came to dominate both culturally and politically no doubt consisted of the more westerly parts of the Iranian plateau including the country later known as Elam. It was in the course of these political activities and their accompanying military campaigns that the Mesopotamian state first came in conflict with the Sumerians. For this primitive and probably nomadic people which may have erupted from either Trans-caucasia or Transcaspia, was pressing upon the districts of

---

[45] The term is useful in spite of the fact that it combines a name which is primarily geographical with one which is primarily linguistic.

[46] Cf. particularly McCown, *SAOC*, xxiii, pp. 36–42.

western Iran, the "buffer" states between the civilized Mesopotamian empire and the barbarians beyond, and these had to be
defended at all costs. In their first encounter there is little
doubt that the Mesopotamian forces with their superior military
technique, were more than a match for the Sumerian hordes.
But, in the long run, it was the mobile primitive Sumerians
who had the advantage over their more civilized sedentary
adversary. Over the years, as captive hostages in Mesopotamian
cities, and as mercenaries in the Mesopotamian armies, the
Sumerian warriors learned what they needed most of the more
advanced military techniques of their captors and hirers. And
as the Mesopotamian power weakened and tottered, the Sumerians poured through the buffer states of western Iran, and invaded Lower Mesopotamia itself, where they took over as
masters and conquerors.[47]

[47] To use the more customary archaeological terminology, the first stage
of the pre-Sumerian period corresponds perhaps to Uruk XVIII–XVII; the
second stage perhaps to Uruk XVI–XV; the third stage perhaps to Uruk
XIV–VIII. The most significant feature of this tentative reconstruction of
the earliest history of Lower Mesopotamia is the assumed existence of a
highly civilized urban state prior to that of the Sumerians; it follows of
course only if the existence of a Sumerian Heroic Age has been correctly
adduced and if its causes and antecedents have been properly analyzed. So
high a civilization naturally implies the existence of monumental architecture in the more important sites of Lower Mesopotamia during the
centuries represented by Uruk XIV–VIII; the pits and shafts excavated to
date are unfortunately non-committal on this all important matter, but cf.
now the prehistoric temples VI and VII excavated at Eridu (*Sumer*, iii. no.
2, pp. 84–111). It is not altogether impossible that this pre-Sumerian civilization may have had some form of writing; however, if the materials used
consisted of such perishable stuff as wood or skin, it may be beyond re-
covery. The hypothesis that the first empire in Lower Mesopotamia was
predominantly Semitic is based in the first place on the later pattern of
Lower Mesopotamian history. Moreover it is not impossible that the Su-
marian king list (cf. now Jacobsen's very useful compilation, *The Sumerian
King List, AS*, xi) which gives for the first dynasty of Kish, that is, the
first dynasty after the flood, a list of kings whose names are in large part
Semitic, reflects a tradition based at least partially on fact (Kish must therefore have existed in the pre-Sumerian period in spite of the present dearth
of archaeological evidence). Finally there are a number of Semitic loan
words in the older Sumerian texts which point to a Semitic speaking people
as the ruling ethnic group immediately preceding the Sumerians; for the

Turning now from the pre-Sumerian, or Irano-Semitic period in the earlier history of Lower Mesopotamia, to the following Sumerian period, the latter, too, is found to consist of three cultural stages, the preliterate, the proto-literate, and the early-literate. The first, or preliterate stage of the Sumerian period, begins with an era of stagnation and regression in the wake of the collapse of the earlier and more advanced Irano-Semitic civilization, and the incursion of the Sumerian barbaric war-bands into Lower Mesopotamia. During these centuries which culminated in the Sumerian Heroic Age, it was the culturally immature and psychologically unstable Sumerian war lords with their highly individualistic and predatory dispositions who held sway over the sacked cities and burnt villages of the first vanquished Mesopotamian empire. Moreover these Sumerian invaders were themselves at first far from secure in their new Mesopotamian habitat. For it would seem that not long after they had made themselves masters in the land, new nomadic hordes from the western desert, Semitic tribes known as the Martu, "who knew not grain"[48], poured into Lower Mesopotamia. As late as the days of Enmerkar and Lugalbanda, that is, in the heyday of the Sumerian Heroic Age, the struggle between these desert barbarians and the but recently "citified" Sumerians was still raging. Under these circumstances it is hardly likely that the times immediately following the arrival of the Sumerian hordes were conducive to progress in the economic and technological fields, or to creative efforts in the fields of art and architecture. Only in the literary field may we assume a marked creative activity on the part of the illiterate court minstrels who were moved to improvise and compose

---

present, cf. Poebel in *ZA*, 39, p. 149, note 2 (Frankfort's argument in *SAOC*, iv, p. 43, is based of course mainly on the assumption that the Sumerians were the first to settle in Lower Mesopotamia). As for the struggle between the civilized pre-Sumerian Mesopotamian power and the Sumerian barbarians settled on its utmost fringes, cf. the pertinent and illuminating parallel instances in the history of civilization gathered by Toynbee in vol. v of his *Study of History*.

[48] Cf. e.g. Langdon, *The H. Weld-Blundell Collection in the Ashmolean Museum* (*OECT*, i) pl. 6, col. ii, line 13.

their oral epic lays for the entertainment of their lords and masters.

It is when we come to the second or proto-literate stage of the Sumerian period we find the Sumerians firmly planted and deeply rooted in their new land; it was perhaps in the course of this cultural phase that the name Sumer first came to be applied to Lower Mesopotamia. By this time the more stable elements of the ruling caste, particularly the court and temple administrators and intellectuals, were coming to the fore. There was now a strong movement for "law and order" in the land, as well as an awakening of the community spirit and patriotic pride. Moreover, the rather unusually fruitful fusion, both ethnic and cultural, of the Sumerian conquerors with the vanquished but more civilized native population, brought about a creative spurt that was fraught with significance not alone for Sumer but for Western Asia as a whole. It was during this cultural stage that architecture was developed to a new high level. And this was the time that probably witnessed the invention of writing, an event which proved to be the decisive factor in molding the Near East into a cultural unit in spite of its diverse and polyglot ethnic elements.[49] For this Sumerian system of writing in its later conventionalized form was borrowed by practically all the more cultured peoples of Western Asia. As a result, the study of the Sumerian language and literature became a major discipline in the narrowly restricted but highly influential "literate" circles of the ancient Near East. It was this leaven of Sumerian achievement on the intellectual and spiritual plane—note that the "Sumerian" achievements were actually the product of at least three ethnic groups, the proto-Iranian, Semitic, and Sumerian—that raised the Near Eastern ethos to a new high point in the early history of civilization.

The last, or early-literate cultural stage of the Sumerian period witnessed the further development and continued maturing of the material and spiritual achievements which originated in the main in the preceding and more creative proto-literate stage. Particularly in the matter of writing, the largely picto-

[49] Cf. particularly Speiser's illuminating comment in *JAOS*, supplement 4, pp. 25–28.

graphic and ideographic script of the preceding era was molded and modified over the years into a thoroughly conventionalized and purely phonetic system of writing; by the end of this period it could already be utilized for even the more complex historical compositions.[50] It is probably during this early-literate stage, or perhaps even towards the end of the preceding proto-literate phase, that strong Sumerian dynasties first came into being. In spite of the constant strife between city and city for the hegemony over Sumer, some of them did succeed, if only for brief intervals, in extending the political boundaries of Sumer considerably beyond Lower Mesopotamia itself. There thus came into being what might be termed the second—and this time predominantly Sumerian—empire in the history of the Near East.[51] Finally, the Sumerian empire, like its presumably

[50] Cf. Thureau Dangin, *Die sumerischen und akkadischen Königsinschriften*, pp. 10–59, 152–156, and Kramer, *Sumerian Mythology*, p. 10 and plate III.

[51] This Sumerian empire may have been every bit as extensive as that attributed to Sargon of Accad or to the Third Dynasty of Ur; cf. e.g. the seven countries listed as under the sway of Lugalannimundu, king of Adab, in the early post-Sumerian text published by Poebel and translated by Güterbock (for references see now Jacobsen, *AS*, xi, p. 102, note 183); they extend from the Zagros or even beyond, to the Mediterranean Sea. As for the approximate date of Lugalannimundu, note that, if the king list is to be trusted at all at this point, his reign preceded by a considerable margin that of UR–UR of Akshak. Even on the assumption of a very considerable over-lapping of the dynasties of Adab, Mari, Kish III–IV, and Akshak, it seems not unreasonable to conclude that Lugalannimundu of Adab preceded UR–UR of Akshak by some one hundred years. Now it is not at all unlikely that this king UR–UR of Akshak is to be identified with ZU–ZU, the king of Akshak who was defeated by Eannatum of Lagash (cf. now Jacobsen, *op. cit.*, p. 18) for according to a verbal suggestion made by Poebel more than ten years ago, UR–UR is to be read ZU(r)-ZU(r), *just as e.g.* UR–šanabi is to be read ZU(r)-sanabi (cf. Poebel, *JAOS*, lvii, p. 54, note 22, where a future study on the subject is alluded to; cf. also Jacobsen in *OIP*, lviii, p. 203; note that, if the identification UR–UR with ZU–ZU proves correct, the synchronistic arrangement of the table at the end of *AS*, xi, will need very considerable revision). Now if Lugalannimundu of Adab preceded UR–UR of Akshak by a century, and if the latter was a contemporary of Eannatum of Lagash, Lugalannimundu should be dated before Ur-Nanse; indeed it is not altogether impossible that he antedates Mesannipadda, the founder of Ur I. Certainly it is not at all unlikely that, in spite of their position in the

(cont'd)

Semite predeccessor, weakened and crumbled. As a result of the continued infiltration into the land, the Semitic Accadians became ever more powerful, until with the reign of Sargon, which may be said to mark the beginning of the Sumero-Accadian period, we come to the close of the Sumerian period.[52]

In conclusion it may prove of value to attempt to assign, ever so roughly to be sure, absolute dates to the cultural stages outlined in the preceding reconstruction of the earliest history of Lower Mesopotamia, particularly since of late a tendency to

---

king list, the dynasties of Awan, Kish II, Hamazi, and Erech II with their incredibly long reigns, not to mention a goodly number of rulers altogether unlisted in the king list, are to be placed between Gilgamesh of Erech I, and Mesannipadda of Ur I. For if the conclusions drawn in the earlier part of this study are correct, the Enmerkar-Lugalbanda-Gilgamesh era is to be identified as the Sumerian Heroic Age, a barbaric form of society flourishing toward the end of the first, or preliterate, stage of the Sumerian period. Ur I, on the other hand, shows Sumerian civilization in a highly mature form; even the system of writing had already progressed to a purely phonetic and conventionalized script. The time interval between these two eras, or more concretely, between Gilgamesh, the hero of Erech, and Mesannipadda, the first ruler of Ur, cannot possibly be some thirty or forty years (cf. the table at the end of *AS*, 11); it is much more likely to be closer to four hundred years. As for the factors which induced the compilers of the king list to enumerate the earlier dynasties in the particular order chosen, and to attribute to them the unusually large number of reigning years, these still remain quite obscure.

[52] In more customary archaeological terminology, the preliterate stage of the Sumerian period corresponds perhaps to Uruk VII-VI; the proto-literate, perhaps to Uruk V-III (the term "proto-literate" was introduced in *OIP*, lviii, p. 8, note 10, where, however, it is made to correspond with Uruk VII-III); the early-literate period corresponds to the early-dynastic (for the three major subdivisions of the latter, cf. especially Frankfort, *OIC*, xx). The most significant feature of this reconstruction of the Sumerian period in the early history of Lower Mesopotamia consists of the treatment of the Enmerkar-Lugalbanda-Gilgamesh era, that is, the larger part of the first half of the first dynasty of Erech, as a barbaric and illiterate Heroic Age, which is to be separated from the days of Ur I and its highly mature and relatively literate civilization by a very considerable time-span, one which includes the entire length of the proto-literate period and approximately the first half of the early-literate (or early-dynastic) stage; cf. the preceding note.

an overlong chronology is again manifesting itself.[53] Let us start with Hammurabi and assign the beginning of his reign to the middle of the eighteenth century B.C.[54] Since the interval between the beginning of Hammurabi's reign and that of Sargon of Accad is approximately five and one half centuries,[55] Sargon's rule began some time about 2300 B.C. If now we attribute some four centuries to the early-literate stage of the Sumerian period,[56] its beginning would reach back to approximately 2700 B.C. The preceding proto-literate stage probably did not last longer than about two centuries,[57] and the barbaric

[53] Cf. especially *OIP*, lviii, pp. 123–135, where the combined length of the Jemdet Nasr (i.e. the period there labelled as proto-literate c and d) and early-literate (i.e. early-dynastic) is estimated to be more than eleven centuries. The calculations in support of this rather unexpectedly long time-span are based on the precarious assumption that the walls of the Sin temple in Khafajah were replastered *annually*, in view of the fact that "annual replastering of the roofs and exposed walls of buildings of this type at the end of each summer in preparation for the winter rains is still a very common routine in the Near East" (*OIP*, lviii, p. 127). But even if this "wall-plastering criterion" were reliable, we might perhaps be not unjustified in assuming a *semi-annual* plastering for so important a building as the Sin temple; the combined length of the Jemdet Nasr and early-literate periods would thus be cut in half, that is, to about five and one half centuries. If we take the Sumerian system of writing into consideration, it seems quite incredible to assume that it took some eleven centuries to evolve from its Jemdet Nasr stage to that exemplified by the inscriptions of Sargon's predecessor and victim, Lugalzaggisi; some five to six centuries would seem to be a far more reasonable estimate.

[54] For a summary of the problems involved and the pertinent references, cf. Sidney Smith, *AJA*, xlix, pp. 17–23. On the data available at present it seems difficult to decide between the conflicting views, and the date 1750 for the beginning of Hammurabi's reign is merely a makeshift compromise which may prove to be some four decades off one way or the other.

[55] Cf. Christian, *AOF*, v, pp. 139–141, and now especially Jacobsen, *AS*, xi, pp. 204–208, and table at the end of *AS*, xi (the overlong *absolute* dates are of no significance for this particular purpose).

[56] The evolution of the Sumerian system of writing from the stage exemplified by the archaic Ur tablets to that exemplified by the Lugalzaggisi inscriptions speaks in favor of this shorter time-span. Note, too, that on the archaeological side, Frankfort, *JRAS*, 1937, p. 337, attributes less than five centuries to the early-dynastic period.

[57] A time-span of two centuries seems to be rather ample for the evolution
(cont'd)

Sumerian Heroic Age which it followed may therefore perhaps be best assigned to the first century of the third millennium
B.C. As for the first arrival of the conquering but primitive Sumerians in Lower Mesopotamia, it must have taken place in the
course of the last quarter of the fourth millennium B.C.[58] If
we further attribute some five to six centuries to the Irano-
Semitic civilization,[59] the first settlements in Lower Mesopotamia may have taken place in the course of the first quarter
of the fourth millennium B.C.

The French archaeologist, André Parrot, was attracted by the
Kramer thesis and chose, as he said, to enlarge upon it.[60] Taking
a broad view, Parrot envisioned a painted-ware culture from the
east that flowed in two great streams into Mesopotamia: one
entered Assyria (Hassuna-Halaf phase), and the other penetrated the lower valley (Eridu-Ubaid phase). Since the immediate source of the painted-ware culture was Iran, Parrot called
this first period Iranian. By the end of this Iranian age, the
Ubaid culture of the south had spread to Assyria, but the intrusion of a new culture (Uruk) of Iranian or Transcaspian origin
forced the retreat and final extinction of the Ubaid. Mainly
because unpainted monochrome pottery was characteristic of
Anatolia, the similar wares of the Uruk culture caused Parrot to
favor a northwestern origin for the people who introduced the
Urak phase. More important, the thought that it must have been
the Sumerians who brought the Uruk culture to Mesopotamia,
and he further believed that the arrival of the Sumerians was
paralleled or closely followed by the coming of Semites from
the west and Hurrians from the north. However, as the Su-

---

of the Sumerian system of writing from its first beginnings to its Jemdet
Nasr stage.

[58] That is, the preliterate state of the Sumerian period, corresponding
perhaps to Uruk VII-VI, began sometime in the last quarter of the fourth
millennium B.C. and ended sometime in the first quarter of the third millennium B.C.

[59] That is, perhaps Uruk XVI-VIII.

[60] A. Parrot, *Archéologie mésopotamienne*, Vol. II, Paris, 1953, pp. 328-331.

merians forged ahead culturally, the others tended to borrow from them. Late in the Uruk period, the Sumerians invented writing, an innovation significant enough to warrant splitting the long Uruk period into two parts. In principle, Parrot thus agreed with others who wished to combine the later Uruk phase with the Jemdet Nasr and call it Protoliterate. Yet, he concluded, Mesopotamian civilization was not the work of one race or one people even though the Sumerians as creators of culture were in the vanguard of the procession.

The excavation of lower levels at Eridu reported in 1948 had changed the picture in the south. Even as early as 1938, pottery discovered at Hajji Muhammad, near Warka, had been recognized as being earlier than, though related to, Ubaid pottery. Then, at Eridu, pottery that was "pre-Ubaid" or "early Ubaid" had been found: this gave a sequence of Eridu-Hajji Muhammad-Ubaid. The Eridu pottery was not only recognized as having Iranian connections, but also had parallels in the pottery of Samarra, in lower Assyria which was Halafian. Combining the pottery discoveries at Eridu with new evidence relating to the continuity of temple architecture on the same site, Joan Oates brought forward new arguments in support of the Frankfort hypothesis that the Sumerians had arrived in the Ubaid period.

However, before we can consider the problem of Eridu, one additional discovery should be mentioned. Geologic evidence published by Lees and Falcon in 1952 had demonstrated that the land at the head of the Persian Gulf was not of recent origin.[61] This was contrary to what had always been assumed, and it meant that scholars must recognize the possibility that the lower valley could have been open to human habitation at a much earlier time than anyone had previously supposed. This fact, along with the arguments for a continuity of culture in the south, are important considerations in the article by Joan Oates reproduced in part below:[62]

[61] G. M. Lees and N. L. Falcon, "The Geographical History of the Mesopotamian Plains," *Geographical Journal* 118 (1952), pp. 24-39.
[62] J. Oates, "Ur and Eridu; the Prehistory," *Iraq*, 22 (1960), pp. 32-50. The quotations used here are from pp. 44-50. Copyright © British School of Archaeology in Iraq. Reprinted by permission of publisher.

ERIDU AND THE SUMERIAN PROBLEM

The implications of the finds at Eridu are far-reaching. One of the most complex problems on which new light has been shed is that of the Sumerians. From the evidence discovered at Eridu it is possible to construct a most convincing case for continuity from the al 'Ubaid period onwards. Such features as the temple plan show this to a striking degree: the cella flanked by lateral chambers, the central free-standing podium or "offering-table" with traces of ritual burning,[63] the burial of ritual objects by the altar,[64] the pilasterniche facade decoration. There is, in fact, little to distinguish Temple VI at Eridu from the temples of the Uruk period at Warka. Apparently the position of the door is not so important as was once believed; a change in position is noted in Temples VI and VII at Eridu, and in Gawra VIII entrances through both the long and short sides occur in different temples in the same level.[65] It would seem that considerations of space are as important as previous custom in this matter. Other temple features found in the 'Ubaid period and in Sumerian times are: libation vessels, fish offerings, opferstätten,[66] the use of the snake symbol, terracotta censers with pierced openings, ritual breakage.[67]

One of the most significant factors in this argument is the

[63] Compare, for example, the Anu Ziggurat at Warka and the Diyala temples.

[64] Sumer IV p. 119, cf. the Abu Temple at T. Asmar; Delougaz and Lloyd, "Pre-Sargonid Temples in the Diyala Region," O.I.P. LVIII, 1942, p. 157 and Fig. 150.

[65] In Temples VII and VIII both end and side entrances to the sanctuary, direct and indirect, exist but in VI the end entrance is no longer in use. It is the latter entrance, however, that is most common in Uruk temples, although side entrances through lateral chambers seem to be the only means of access to the 'Uqair Painted Temple. Sumer III Figs. 2, 3; Sumer IV Pl. VI; J.N.E.S. II, 1943, Lloyd and Safar ('Uqair), Pl. V.

[66] Eridu Temples XVII, XVI; see Sumer IV Pl. VI. See also Mrs. Van Buren, Iraq XIV, 1952, pp. 76–92, especially pp. 83–4.

[67] Compare the broken libation vessels of Eridu with the ritually broken cups of the Abu Temple, T. Asmar; Delougaz and Lloyd, op. cit., p. 166.

method of building the temple platform. Temple VI stood on a raised platform beyond the limits of which it was possible to distinguish no less than five concentric rectangles of masonry representing successive extensions of the platform. "The surviving chambers of Temple VI were found, from their pavement upwards, to be packed out solid with *libn* which suggested that the preparations for building a new temple consisted, not only in extending the platform laterally, but also increasing its height so that the walls of the old temple were incorporated in its fabric."[68] Here we have an indubitable example, not only of continuity from 'Ubaid to Uruk temples, but also of an attitude toward the preservation of the earlier foundations which can only be explained in the light of a persistence of religious beliefs. The ultimate purpose was obviously to protect the earlier foundations from defilement and at the same time to preserve them as "religious relics." This same idea can be seen in the construction of the Anu Ziggurat at Warka and of the Diyala temples.[69]

Another important piece of evidence at Eridu is the further substantiation of the architectural continuity between early and late Uruk. As Seton Lloyd points out, "It is significant that amongst the debris from which the later group of Uruk pottery is derived, though no cylinder seals or tablets are present, many familiar features of "post-Warka VI" architecture are to be found. They include *Schtiften Mosaik, Siegelabrollungen auf Gips*, cement bricks, bricks pierced for applied ornament, and mosaic fragments of coloured stone, pierced for attachment."[70]

As we have already seen, the ceramic evidence also suggests cultural continuity; the changes within the painted pottery series at Eridu are consonant with what one might expect over

[68] *Sumer* III, p. 103.

[69] This habit of preserving the sacred remains of earlier temples is connected psychologically with another feature characteristic of temple building in Mesopotamia, the desire to build without deviation according to previously set precedents. A classic example is, of course, the building of a temple to Ningirsu at Lagash by Gudea. See Mrs. Van Buren, *Or.* 21, 1952, p. 293, for the building of temples in conformity with the "ordinances and ritual of Eridu."

[70] Lloyd, "Uruk Pottery," *Sumer* IV, 1948, p. 51.

a period of time in any pottery sequence. The same is true of the transition to the Uruk period when undecorated ware is predominant, and the new red and grey wares, which appear in the latest 'Ubaid levels, are found in larger quantity.

Most authorities would argue the arrival of the Sumerians either at the beginning of the 'Ubaid or in the Uruk period, and most agree that the later Uruk period is too late. The suggestion that Sumerian civilization was a linear descendant of the al 'Ubaid culture has not hitherto been universally accepted, since until the excavation of Eridu the arguments on either side rested too heavily on fragmentary evidence and hypothesis. Eridu has now supplied positive evidence of continuity, not only in the pottery sequence, which is perhaps open to more than one interpretation, but also in religion. It is extremely difficult to believe that the location of the temple, its cult, and even its architecture would have continued in an unbroken tradition from al 'Ubaid to Sumerian times if there had been during this period any major change in the character of the population. It is unnecessary here to reiterate the other arguments for cultural continuity from the 'Ubaid period onwards, which have been put forward ably and at length by others;[71] but it is important to note that the term "Sumerian," although by strict definition linguistic, is generally used to describe the common culture of a population composed of mixed linguistic elements, and there is some reason to suppose that its ethnic composition was equally diverse. From the time of the earliest records, there appears to be no social distinction in Sumer between persons bearing Semitic and Sumerian names,[72] and it has been suggested that some of the place-names derive from

[71] A useful summary of these arguments is to be found in Speiser, "The Sumerian Problem Reviewed." *Hebrew Union College Annual* XXIII, 1950–51, pp. 339–355.

[72] See Jacobsen, "The Assumed Conflict between Sumerians and Semites in early Mesopotamian History," *J.A.O.S.* 59, 1939, pp. 485–95; also Gelb, "Old Akkadian Writing and Grammar," *M.A.D.* II, 1952, pp. 5–7. The numerical predominance of Sumerian personal names at this time seems to show conclusively that the language was not a recent introduction.

yet another linguistic source. Moreover, the supposedly "Sumerian" physical type is conventional in the sculpture of Mari, among a population whose names are largely Semitic. What we do not know, of course, is to what extent it is conventional in Sumer, where there appears to be a marked discrepancy between the appearance of the Sumerians as depicted on the monuments and the available evidence of physical type. Since we cannot recognise any intrusive element among this medley, it seems probable that we must attribute it to a mingling of stocks in prehistoric times, and this must be taken into account in attempting to reconstruct the history of the early periods.

We have seen that the evidence from Eridu suggests a continuous development from the very earliest levels throughout the Uruk period. At no point is there any indication of a foreign "invasion," and there is no innovation that cannot be explained in terms of normal cultural growth. One of the strongest arguments in favour of discontinuity, what has been called the "drastic break" in pottery styles, would seem to be erroneous. This, of course, raises the question of the origins of the earliest "Eridu" people. At present we know of no other culture from which theirs can be derived. As pointed out previously; the closest parallels are to Samarra in the north. Both Samarra and "Eridu," particularly the former, show some degree of affinity with early Iranian cultures in Fars, none of which, however, is chronologically as early as the Mesopotamian groups; the earliest ceramic known from the Marv Dasht plain seems quite dissimilar to either Mesopotamian ware.[73] No other Iranian ceramic is known from which either Samarra or "Eridu" can be derived, Samarra analogies to the Sialk I *céramique claire* being extremely slight. Although we cannot deny the possibility of an Iranian origin for the Mesopotamian cultures in question, there is certainly no positive evidence to support this hypothesis. On the contrary the develop-

[73] Vanden Berghe, "Archaeologische Opzoekingen in de Marv Dasht Vlakte (Iran)," *Jaarbericht Ex Oriente Lux* 12, 1952; see also Vanden Berghe, *Archéologie de l'Iran Ancien*, 1959, pp. 41–2 and Pl. 49.

ment of the Samarra style within the general Hassuna range is quite in keeping with the evidence both from Hassuna and Matarrah.[74]

It was long assumed that the early cultures of Southern Mesopotamia must derive from elsewhere, since the land itself was believed to be of comparatively recent, deltaic origin. This has now been disproved by the work of Lees and Falcon,[75] and a fresh approach to the problem is possible. The new geological theory combined with the lack of evidence for a foreign origin of the Eridu pottery leads one to suspect the existence of earlier settlements in Sumer proper. These, however, if they do exist, may well prove very difficult to detect. Surface indications of such small settlements, now covered by layers of sand and silt and perhaps even by the marshes themselves, are not likely to exist, and the discovery of this type of occupation beneath larger and later villages would be a matter of luck. The problem is further complicated by the fact that the rising water table has prevented excavation to virgin soil at a number of southern sites. If the sand at Eridu is merely a dune, there remains the possibility of earlier occupation at that site. It would be useful to know the absolute elevation of the Eridu sand deposit, as at nearby Ur the earliest settlement was on marshy ground not far above present sea level. Similar marsh-like conditions were found beneath the earliest excavated occupation levels at Warka and 'Uqair. Heinrich describes the lowest level at Warka, which was penetrated for only half a

---

[74] See Braidwood, "Matarrah: A Southern Variant of the Hassunan Assemblage," *J.N.E.S.* XI, 1952, p. 4.

[75] G. M. Lees and N. L. Falcon, "The Geographical History of the Mesopotamian Plains," *Geographical Journal* CXVIII, 1952. This is not an entirely new theory. Similar though less complete evidence was presented by Sir Arnold Wilson as early as 1925. ("The Delta of the Shatt al 'Arab and Proposals for Dredging the Bar," *Geographical Journal* LXV, 1925) In 1920 Campbell Thompson wrote, in reference to the occurrence of shells in his excavations at Eridu, "I think that the freshwater mussel shells which I found in great quantity in different strata, when taken into consideration with the very few finds of marine shells, will compel us to give up the idea that Eridu was in ancient times actually on the sea-shore." (*Archaeologia* LXX, p. 124.)

metre, as consisting of a bright green distinctly layered clay like the wet ground of the present-day Hor an Najaf.[76] This deposit contained some sherds, an indication that there had been human occupation in the area previous to its deposition (as there was at nearby Hajji Muhammad), whereas the equivalent green clay at Ur was said to have contained no potsherds or other evidence of human life. One would expect to find early occupation in and near the marshes which would have provided an excellent food and water supply. The areas of marsh and lake have, of course, shifted in the course of time,[77] which would explain the drying up of the marshes or lagoons which once must have existed near Ur and Warka.

The probability of earlier occupation in the south is strengthened by the fact that the extent of the Hajji Muhammad occupation is far wider than was first suspected. There is evidence of a settlement of this date at Nippur, and a Hajji Muhammad village is known to exist near Kish.[78] Also, the "Eridu" settlements in the vicinity of the type site were obviously fairly extensive. At 'Usaila, a part of the Eridu depression about eight kilometres northwest of Eridu, are a group of small *tells*, on at least three of which occurs surface material of Eridu-Hajji Muhammad type. Others have mainly a mixture of Hajji Muhammad and later 'Ubaid.[79]

Although the evidence is far too scanty to justify any positive conclusions, some relevant considerations may be put forward. Firstly, the Sumerian analogy suggests that we are not dealing, in the al 'Ubaid period, with a homogeneous population. We must think, rather, of a culture which became homogeneous by the combination and assimilation of diverse earlier elements. An example of such diversity may be found, although the point

---

[76] *U.V.B.* IV, 1932, p. 6.

[77] There is, for example, evidence that the great Hor al Hammar marsh between Ur and Basra only came into existence in about A.D. 600. Le Strange, *J.R.A.S.* XXVII, 1895, p. 297, and *Lands of the Eastern Caliphate*, 1930, p. 27.

[78] Nippur: a brief sounding in the 1952 season. A sounding has just been made at Kish site by Mr. David Stronach for The British School of Archaeology in Iraq.

[79] I am indebted to Sayid Fuad Safar for this information.

cannot be proved, in the different burial customs of the 'Ubaid and Uruk inhabitants of Ur. The change from extended to flexed inhumation represents, perhaps, some slight variation in belief about the after-life, or merely in community tradition, which disappeared during the process of coagulation which produced the later, standardized culture. Whatever the explanation of this particular change may be, it does not necessarily imply the replacement of one homogeneous population with its own array of beliefs and customs, by another; in conditions of growing prosperity and cultural advancement, one would expect an increase in the indigenous population and a gradual rapprochement between neighbouring communities whose habits and way of life may originally have differed. Such a situation is commonplace in Western Europe, where the overall pattern of culture in Neolithic or Chalcolithic times is composed of many elements, clearly in contact with and influencing one another, but at different stages of cultural evolution and of diverse origins. The study of Mesopotamian prehistory has perhaps suffered overmuch from the anxiety of archaeologists to trace the evolution of civilization as a single Darwinian process, for such an approach often blinds us to the complexity, and the geographical variety, of early society.

We should not, however, replace the unsatisfactory concept of Darwinian evolution with an equally dangerous assumption, that the dominant traits of which we have evidence in a composite culture, must of necessity have been contributed by that segment of the population which lived by a "superior," i.e. agricultural, economy. This may very well be true in areas where farming obviously yields a greater economic surplus than hunting, fishing, and food-gathering; but in the particular instance with which we are concerned, the environment of Southern Mesopotamia, the very profitable agriculture of historic times depended on advanced techniques of irrigation, which pre-suppose a measure of political unity over large areas. The work of Lees and Falcon has demonstrated that we must envisage a physical environment not greatly different from that which exists today, and particularly in the marshes there were probably communities which gained as profitable a livelihood from hunting and fishing as did their neighbours from herding and primitive agriculture. In fact, we should be prepared to find traces, in pre-'Ubaid or pre-"Eridu" times, of more than one type of indigenous community, differing from one another in material culture and perhaps even in physical type and in language, although the second point will be difficult and the last impossible to verify. Some of these communities may well have been "proto-Sumerian." Certainly the most able protagonists of the theory of a "Sumerian invasion" have never been able to identify the hypothetical homeland from which these people, with their unique language and distinctive culture, are alleged to have come, and this failure becomes the more damaging to their case as our archaeological knowledge of the lands bordering on Mesopotamia increases. Certain traits in the later and more widely diffused culture will no doubt be found to have come from outside the area, whether by contact with other peoples or by an actual movement of population; but even here we must beware of too hasty conclusions, as a brief consideration of the question of painted pottery will show. It is *prima facie* unlikely that the decoration of pottery or other objects with pigments such as haematite originated in Southern Mesopotamia, where the materials would always have been imported, and in the earliest levels we may well find unpainted wares. But it would be false to assume that the motifs of "Eridu" were introduced from elsewhere, since they may have been employed long before on perishable materials such as basketry; and when we remember that one of the principal exports of the Marsh Arab communities at the present day is reed matting, we cannot claim that the surplus wealth necessary for the purchase of imported pigments was not available before the introduction of agriculture. It is tempting to see some confirmation of the role which may have been played by the marsh-dwelling communities in the formation of al 'Ubaid-Sumerian culture, in the traditional temple offerings at Eridu and Lagash. The finds at Eridu, and at a considerably later period at Lagash, show that in these places the people dedicated to Enki his portion of their goods, not in the form of grain or meat, the basic form of wealth among farming communities, but in fish, the product of river, lagoon, and marsh—a tradition which is hardly likely to have been derived from a population principally dependent on the success of their fields and flocks.

An investigation of the sites which are known to exist in the present marsh areas would throw much light on this question; although only the tops of the mounds are at present above water level, the pottery found on these islands goes back at least to the Isin-Larsa period, and of course we have no means of knowing what the lower strata might yield. It is not, however, our intention here to stress unduly the importance of any element in the pre-'Ubaid cultures, since the number, nature, and origin of these elements is entirely a matter of speculation, and a new body of facts is our most urgent need. The evidence as it stands suggests that the civilization of Southern Mesopotamia owes comparatively little, where formerly it was believed to owe everything, to foreign invaders; and the earlier interpretation has been found to rest on entirely false geographical premises. When a new material becomes available, we must try to avoid formulating a new set of unjustified assumptions.

We may conclude this section with a "modern" overview of the Sumerian Problem that probably is representative of the scholarly consensus today:[80]

THE SUMERIAN PROBLEM

Who are these Sumerians, whose name can now be pronounced for the first time and who are going to occupy the stage of history for the next thousand years? Do they represent a very ancient layer of population in prehistoric Mesopotamia, or did they come from some other country, and if so, when did they come and whence? This important problem has been

[80] G. Roux, *Ancient Iraq*, (London and New York: George Allen & Unwin Ltd. and The World Publishing Company, 1966,) pp. 82–85. Copyright © George Allen & Unwin Ltd. 1964. Reprinted by permission of the publisher. Finally, the sequence of prehistoric cultures now seems to be less clearcut than was formerly supposed. On this point, see Joan Oates, "Prehistoric Investigations near Mahdali, Iraq," *Iraq* XXX (1968), pp. 1–20.

debated again and again ever since the first relics of the Sumerian civilization were brought to light nearly a century ago, and is still with us. The most recent discoveries, far from offering a solution, have made it even more difficult to answer, but at least they have supplied fresh and solid arguments to an old debate and it is in this new light that the 'Sumerian problem' should be examined.

The word "Sumerian" comes from the ancient name of the southern part of Iraq: *Sumer* or, more exactly, *Shumer*, usually written in cuneiform texts with the signs KI. EN. GI. At the beginning of historical times three ethnic groups lived in close contact within that region: the Sumerians, predominant in the extreme south from approximately Nippur (near Diwaniyah) to the Persian Gulf—the Semites, predominant in central Mesopotamia (the region called *Akkad* after 2400 B.C.)—and a small, diffuse minority of uncertain origin to which no definite label can be attached. From the point of view of the modern historian, the line of demarcation between these three components of the first historical population of Mesopotamia is neither political nor cultural but linguistic. All of them had the same institutions; all of them shared the way of life, the techniques, the artistic traditions, the religious beliefs, in a word the civilization which had originated in the extreme south and is rightly attributed to the Sumerians, The only reliable criterion by which we can separate and identify these three peoples is therefore their language. *Stricto sensu*, the appellation "Sumerians" should be taken as meaning "Sumerian-speaking people" and nothing else; similarly, the "Semites" were those who spoke a Semitic dialect; and indeed we would be unaware of the existence of the third ethnic element were it not for a few strange, non-Sumerian and non-Semitic personal names and place names which occur here and there in ancient texts. This, incidentally, explains why all efforts to define and to assess the relations between Sumerians and Semites in other fields than philology are doomed to failure. Another point should be made quite clear: there is no such thing as a Sumerian 'race' neither in the scientific nor in the ordinary sense of the term. The skulls from Sumerian graves that have been examined are either dolicho-or brachycephalic and indicate a mixture of the so-called Armenoid and Mediterranean races, the latter being somewhat predominant. As for the physical features depicted on monuments, they are largely conventional and have therefore no real value. The big, fleshy nose, the enormous eyes, the thick neck and flat occiput long considered to be typical of the Sumerians also belong to the statues of individuals bearing genuine Semitic names found in the almost exclusively Semitic district of Mari, while more realistic portraits, such as those of Gudea, the Sumerian governor of Sumerian Lagash, show a short, straight nose and a long head.

Philology alone is often a good index of ethnic relationship. Thus the Greeks, the Hittites and the Indo-Aryans, though dispersed over a wide area, were related to each other through the Indo-European langauges they spoke and probably came from a common homeland in south-eastern Europe. But in the case of the Sumerians philology is of no help. The Sumerian language is "agglutinative," which means that it is formed of verbal radicals modified or inter-connected by the apposition of grammatical particles. As such, it belongs to the same category as numerous dialects spoken from Hungary to Polynesia, though it bears no close resemblance to any known language, dead or living. The Sumerian literature presents us with the picture of a highly intelligent, industrious, argumentative and deeply religious people, but offers no clue as to its origins. Sumerian myths and legends are almost invariably drawn against a background of rivers and marshes, of reeds, tamarisks and palm-trees—a typical southern Iraqi background—as though the Sumerians had always lived in that country, and there is nothing in them to indicate clearly an ancestral homeland different from Mesopotamia.

We are therefore obliged to fall back on archaeology, that is to say on the material elements of the Sumerian civilization. The question here is: which of the various ethnic groups responsible for the successive proto-historic cultures of Mesopotamia can be identified with the Sumerian-speaking people of history? Put in this way the problem is of course insoluble, since we do not know what languages were spoken in Mesopotamia before the Uruk period. Whatever answer is given can only rest on broad generalization, intuitive thinking or mere guesswork. On this question scholars in general are divided into two groups: for some the Sumerians came to Mesopotamia during the Uruk period: for others they were already there in Ubaid times at the latest. We cannot enter here into a detailed discussion, but we are personally rather inclined to agree with the tenets of the second theory. True, the Sumerian *writing* appears for the first time at the end of the Uruk period, but this does not imply that the Sumerian language was not spoken before. Again, there are in ancient Mesopotamia literature place names that are neither Sumerian nor Semitic, but do they necessarily represent the traces of an older and *exclusive* population? As for the change in pottery style which marks the beginning of the Uruk period, who can say with certainty whether it was brought about by invasion, foreign influence or a purely local change of fashion? In fact, in all respects except pottery, the Uruk culture appears as the development of conditions that existed during the Ubaid period. The persistence of religious traditions throughout, in particular, is remarkable. To take only one example among many, the thick layer of fish bones which covered the floor of the Ubaid temples at Eridu offers a near certitude that the deity worshipped there was already the Sumerian water-god Enki.

Can we go farther back into the past? If we accept ceramics as a reliable criterion, the Ubaid folk appear to have come from Iran, and other signs indicate that, at least in the north of Iraq, they behaved as conquerors and imposed their law upon older populations. The "Eridu ware," on the other hand, suggests that the first inhabitants of the south were in some way related to both the Ubaidians and the northern Halafians, as though these were two branches from the same stock. And the Halafians in turn may well have descended from the Neolithic farmers of Hassuna and Jarmo. Thus the more we try to push back the limits of our problem, the more it thins out and vanishes in the mist of prehistory. One is even tempted to wonder whether there is any problem at all. The Sumerians were, as we all are, a mixture of races and probably of peoples;

their civilization, like ours, was a blend of foreign and indigenous elements; their language belongs to a linguistic group large enough to have covered the whole of Western Asia and much more. They may therefore represent a branch of the population which occupied the greater part of the Near East in early Neolithic and Chalcolithic times. In other words, they may have "always" been in Iraq, and this is all we can say. As one of the most brilliant orientalists put it: "The much discussed problem of the origin of the Sumerians may well turn out to be the chase of a chimera."

CONCLUSION

No one has ever said, or is likely to say for years to come, the last word on the Sumerian Problem. Every hypothesis so far advanced has been based on an accumulation of evidence up to a particular moment. And in every case, this evidence has been shown to be woefully incomplete.

The fragmentary pieces of the puzzle that we now possess seem to admit of two hypothetical constructions of the whole: (1) that the Sumerians were present at the beginning of the peasant village stage (Eridu) or (2) that they arrived during the Uruk period. If we accept the philological arguments of Speiser and Landsberger, the Sumerians were *not* the first settlers; if we incline to the archaeological interpretation of the Eridu material, we must conclude that the Sumerians *were* the first arrivals.[1]

[1] A third view, briefly stated and without elaborate documentation, may be found in A. Leo Oppenheim, *Letters from Mesopotamia*, Chicago 1967, pp. 18-21. Accepting the linguistic argument for pre-Sumerian habitation of the lower valley, Oppenheim makes the point that the cuneiform system "does not adequately fit the Sumerian language." This is intended to mean that the system was invented for writing a non-Sumerian language and was subsequently borrowed, but not perfectly adapted, by the Sumerians for their own use. Oppenheim has said elsewhere (*Ancient Mesopotamia*, Chicago 1964, p. 238) that "the inherited polyvalence of certain signs"—their polyphonic property—is a "telltale" indication "of the transfer from a non-Sumerian language to Sumerian."

As for the date when the Sumerians entered the lower valley, Professor Oppenheim says (*Letters from Mesopotamia*, p. 20): ". . . . with the Sumerians a new element had arrived. . . . This is possibly corroborated by a break in the sequence of archeologically determined phases in the first third millennium." What "break in the sequence" in the period 3000-2660 B.C. he has in mind Oppenheim does not specify. It is possibly that between Early Dynastic I and Early Dynastic II.

For a diametrically opposed view, see C. J. Gadd, "The Cities of Babylonia," *Cambridge Ancient History* (rev. ed.), Vol. I, fasc. 34, Cambridge, Eng., 1962, pp. 1-5.

But if past experience is any criterion, there is more to come! What are some of the possibilities? The discovery of pre-Eridu remains in the south might tend either to confirm or destroy the theory of Sumerian primacy with regard to occupation. Excavation outside Mesopotamia might disclose the homeland of the Sumerians—assuming that they were invaders of the lower valley. Without linguistic evidence, this would be difficult to establish, although the survival of place names with Sumerian etymologies would be a clue. That such a thing is possible can be suggested by a purely (and wildly) hypothetical example:

We know very little about the Indus civilization or its antecedents. We cannot read the Indus script and so do not know who the Indus people were or what language they spoke. If the Indus script were to be deciphered and if, through decipherment, it was learned that the oldest town names had Sumerian etymologies, we should be likely to assume that the Sumerians had once lived in the Indus region, and we should explore the possibility of their having migrated from the Indus to the Tigris-Euphrates valley. As far as the Sumerian Problem was concerned, the identity of the people who lived in the Indus region during the civilized period (2500–1500 B.C.) would not be of the first importance since it would merely be through their documents that we should learn of Sumerian priority of habitation in their country.

Regardless of future discoveries, however, as the Sumerian Problem stands at present we cannot be absolutely certain that either the philological or archaeological "evidence" is of a kind that *must* be used in the way in which scholars have chosen to use it. Evidence it is, but of what? The future may show that we have been almost as naïve as Eduard Meyer with his three physical types and costumes.

Poor Halévy fell by the wayside, but in principle he did not err.

SELECT BIBLIOGRAPHY

Cambridge Ancient History, Vol. I. Cambridge University Press: Cambridge, England, 1923.

Fossey, Charles, *Manuel d'Assyriologie*, Vol. I. Ernest Leroux: Paris, 1904.

Frankfort, Henri, "Archeology and the Sumerian Problem," *Oriental Institute Studies in Ancient Oriental Civilization*, No. 4. Chicago University Press: Chicago 1932.

Gadd, C.J., "The Cities of Babylonia," *Cambridge Ancient History* (rev. ed.), Vol I, fasc. 34. Cambridge University Press: Cambridge, England, 1962.

Hilprecht, H.V., *The Excavations in Assyria and Babylonia*. University of Pennsylvania Press: Philadelphia, 1904.

Jastrow, Morris, *The Civilization of Babylonia and Assyria*. J. P. Lippincott: Philadelphia, 1915.

Jones, Tom B., *Paths to the Ancient Past*. Free Press: New York, 1967.

King, Leonard W., *History of Sumer and Akkad*. Chatto and Windus: London, 1910.

Kramer, Samuel Noah, *The Sumerians*. University of Chicago Press: Chicago, 1963.

Mallowan, M.E.L., *Early Mesopotamia and Iran*. Thames and Hudson: London, 1965.

Mellaart, James, *Earliest Civilizations of the Near East*. Thames and Hudson: London, 1965.

Parrot, André, *Archéologie Mésopotamienne*, 2 vols. Albin Michel: Paris, 1946-1953.

Perkins, Ann L., "The Comparative Archaeology of Early Mesopotamia," *Oriental Institute Studies in Ancient Oriental Civilization*, No. 25. University of Chicago Press: Chicago, 1949.

Roux, Georges, *Ancient Iraq*. Penguin Books, Ltd.: Harmondsworth, Middlesex, England, 1966.

Speiser, Ephraim A., *Mesopotamian Origins*. University of Pennsylvania Press: Philadelphia, 1930.

Woolley, C. Leonard, *The Sumerians*. Oxford University Press: Oxford, 1928.